MIKE CRONIN

Doesn't Time Fly?

Aer Lingus – Its History

The Collins Press

First published in 2011 by
The Collins Press
West Link Park
Doughcloyne
Wilton
Cork

British Library Cataloguing in Publication data

Cronin, Mike.
   Doesn't time fly? : Aer Lingus - its history.
   1. Aer Lingus--History. 2. Aeronautics, Commercial--
   Ireland--History.
   I. Title
   387.7'065417-dc22

ISBN-13: 9781848891111

Design and typesetting by Anú Design, Tara
Typeset in Bembo
Printed in Italy by Printer Trento

Contents

Acknowledgements

All writers of history stand on the shoulders of those who have gone before. This is particularly true in this case, and I must acknowledge the excellent material that I have used extensively to recreate the narrative that surrounds the airline, and which was available from two of the previous works charting the history of Aer Lingus, namely Bernard Share, *The Flight of the Iolar: The Aer Lingus Experience, 1936–86* (Dublin, 1986) and Niall G. Weldon, *Pioneers in Flight: Aer Lingus and the Story of Aviation in Ireland* (Dublin, 2002). At Aer Lingus I have been given invaluable help and guidance by Declan Kearney and Gillian Culhane, while Linda Crowe has assisted in providing all manner of material from within the company. Declan and Gillian made themselves readily available, and also gave me access to the many riches that lie within the company archive. They also provided a series of key introductions to those who have worked for the company over the decades. Eamon Power, a lifelong Aer Lingus employee, gave freely of his time and in-depth knowledge, and made sure that all was correct. The insight of Linda King, of IADT, Dun Laoghaire, and her incredible knowledge was vital in helping me understand design issues and the advertising of Aer Lingus. In particular, her chapter '(De)Constructing the Tourist Gaze: Dutch Influences on Aer Lingus Posters, 1950–1960' in Linda King and Elaine Sission, eds, *Ireland, Design and Visual Culture: Negotiating Modernity, 1922–92* (Cork, 2011), was invaluable.

At Boston College, all my colleagues at the Centre for Irish Programmes were as supportive and helpful as ever, and in our Irish branch, the ongoing expertise, assistance and support of Arlene Crampsie, Mark Duncan, Regina Fitzpatrick, Thea Gilien, Claire McGowan, Paul Rouse and Ben Shorten was deeply appreciated. Eoghan Clear, for his usual enthusiasm for interesting happenings, is, as always, an inspiration. For material collected from beyond Aer Lingus' own archive, I have to acknowledge those artefacts offered to me by airline staff, past and present, as well as images from the Aer Lingus collection at the National Archives of Ireland. At the National Archives, the help of Brian Donnelly was invaluable, and his time spent with me in a cold January storage area much appreciated. Peter Rigney, at the Irish Railway Record Society, was a mine of information and made the files relating to the establishment and early years of the airline available to me. Having been fortunate enough to have worked with them before, I was thankful again for the professionalism and vision of the staff of The Collins Press, as well as the team at Anú Design.

Finally, at home, I have to thank my family – Moynagh, Ellen and Samson – for their endless love and support, which means the world to me. However, I think the latter enjoyed the research on this book more than the others. To a young boy, endless photographs of planes lying around the house proved far more interesting than the usual research material Dad brings home!

Mike Cronin
Dublin, 2011

v

Nomenclature

Throughout the text, the airline is referred to simply as Aer Lingus. This has been done to avoid confusion, as the airline has functioned, since 1936, under a variety of company names, and the planes, depending on route, have featured a variety of fuselage markings. Broadly, these are as follows:

1936:	Aer Lingus Teoranta is registered as a company to run Ireland's airline.
1936–1944:	Planes are marked only with the designator EI. In publicity for pre-war services the airline is often advertised as 'Irish Sea Airways, operated by Blackpool and West Coast Air Services & Aer Lingus Teoranta'.
1944–1965:	Planes on Irish and European routes are marked 'Aer Lingus'.
1947:	Aerlínte Éireann is registered as a company to run the transatlantic route.
1958–1965:	All transatlantic planes marked 'Aer Lingus Irish International'.
1965–1974:	Entire fleet marked 'Aer Lingus Irish'.
1974–Present:	Entire fleet marked 'Aer Lingus'.

Preface

The history of Aer Lingus and the nation of Ireland are in many ways inter-twined. From the beginning of the twentieth century, Ireland has made its mark on the world of aviation, from being the landing point for the first transatlantic flight to being a centre for global aviation leasing. As a small island nation, Ireland has punched way above our weight in this respect.

Since the first Aer Lingus aircraft, the 'Iolar', took to the skies in 1936, Aer Lingus has contributed either economically, socially or culturally throughout every period of Ireland's development. Throughout the subsequent decades we have always focussed on our main purpose: connecting Ireland with the world.

So often the first sight of the familiar Aer Lingus shamrock, seen on the tail of our aircraft at airports across the world, has delivered a reassuring sense of homecoming for so many Irish people.

Of course, Aer Lingus has always been at the centre of the far-flung Irish diaspora. It has carried many Irish emigrants to begin their new lives abroad and thankfully has welcomed many other emigrants back home again.

Through promoting travel into and out of Ireland and carrying many millions of customers over the years, Aer Lingus has in its own way contributed to the famous openness and outward looking nature of the Irish nation and people.

Many thousands of Aer Lingus staff past and present have dedicated their working lives to being proud ambassadors for their company and country. Throughout our seventy-five year history, they have worn their uniform with pride and delivered the renowned Aer Lingus service to all our customers.

I am proud to be Chief Executive of this great airline, an airline that has played an important part in putting Ireland on the world stage. This book seeks to capture the rich history and values of our company that this year celebrates seventy-five years. I am sure you will enjoy each page of this wonderful book as much as I shall.

Happy 75th Birthday Aer Lingus.

Christoph Mueller, Chief Executive, Aer Lingus, May 2011

Courtesy of Captain Dara Campbell.

Introduction

The airline business of the twenty-first century is a cut-throat affair. The entry of budget airlines into the market changed the business dramatically, and external factors such as oil prices, wars, weather and even ash clouds from volcanoes can tip the balance of an airline's budget sheet from profit to loss in the matter of weeks. The history of aviation is littered with the names of airlines that have gone out of business. Ireland has a proud history of aviation, from its early fliers, its central role in transatlantic flight and as the home of the budget airline concept. Most central to all these stories, especially given the challenges that have been faced over the decades in the industry, is Aer Lingus: Ireland's national airline. What started in 1936 as an airline with one plane, one route and an inaugural flight for only five people has transformed itself into a major international business. Aer Lingus has dealt with many challenges over its lifetime, and has not only survived but prospered. Its shamrock livery is recognisable all over the world, and it is held in high esteem in the world of aviation.

As the airline celebrates and moves forward from its seventy-fifth year, this book examines how the airline has developed. This is not simply the story of an airline, but also that of the nation it represents, as well as the people who have worked for Aer Lingus and the passengers who have flown with them. The book looks at the early years of flight in Ireland and explains how Aer Lingus began. It tells how the airline's routes have opened up and developed, and details the planes that have flown the shamrock around the world. People *x*

come to the fore as the histories of those who worked for the airline are told, and the relationship between passenger and Aer Lingus uncovered. Aer Lingus has functioned as more than just an airline however. It grew to be a complex, diversified business that offered a range of services from engineering to health care, innovated in the area of information technology and trained airline personnel from around the world. Through its activities, Aer Lingus made Ireland a key player in the aviation industry, and its former staff can be found running major airlines in many countries. What is clear from exploring Aer Lingus' history is that the airline has never stood still. It has been a driver of change within its own organisation and in the broader aviation industry, and it has been challenged by external forces that have, at times, driven it to the brink of extinction. The key strength of the airline is that it has met all those challenges, and continues to fly the tourist, the business person, the VIP, the homebound emigrant and plain old you and me on its routes. This is the story of Aer Lingus, of Ireland in the skies.

1 Beginnings

'Flight is the only truly new sensation that men have achieved in modern history.'

James Dickey

Anyone arriving at a major city airport in the world today, and who looks up at the departures board, will share a familiar sense of possibility. In return for the price of a ticket, we can jet off across the oceans to all five continents. Many of us, privileged enough to do so, now take flying for granted, and what was once seen as impossible, is now part of the everyday. Yet little over a century ago, on 17 December 1903, Orville Wright piloted the first powered airplane 20 feet above a windswept beach in North Carolina. The flight only lasted 12 seconds and covered a distance of barely 120 feet. From Wright's first flight, the rate of development in aviation was breathtaking. What was at first seen as a modern wonder, an almost impossible feat, flying became the stuff of storybook adventure. Early pilots set themselves challenges of distance, speed and endurance and were, in the 1920s and 1930s, global celebrities. The commercial opportunities afforded by flight were quickly identified, and the post-First World War era saw the emergence of passenger-carrying flights in the United States and Europe. That Ireland, a country that had emerged from a period of revolution and civil war at the start of the 1920s, gaining its independence in 1922, was able to join this elite band of commercial aviators by 1936 stands as testament to the vision of the founding fathers of Aer Lingus.

The dream of taking to the skies, and flying like a bird, was one that obsessed men over the centuries. From Archytas, an ancient Greek who it is claimed built and flew a bird-like structure he named the pigeon, through Leonardo da Vinci and his 1485 designs for a human-powered Ornithopter that would be driven through the skies by a mechanical wing, history is littered with plans, models and planes that were designed or built, and yet never made a flight.

3

Here, Harry Ferguson is shown piloting the plane in which, on 31 December 1909, he had successfully completed the first powered aeroplane flight in Ireland. Although he only flew some 130 yards, Ferguson can claim the title of the father of Irish aviation. Despite his early enthusiasm and his role in founding the Irish Aero Club in November 1909, he decided to give up such a potentially dangerous hobby when he married in 1913. However, his mechanical enthusiasm continued and he made his fortune producing the tractors that now carry his name.

It took until the eighteenth century before men made it off the ground and into the air. These early successes depended on a rethinking of what it meant to fly. Whereas earlier designers of airborne vehicles were driven by the belief that success would be achieved by duplicating the abilities of birds, the scientific advancements of the eighteenth century, particularly the understanding of chemical elements, allowed inventors to re-imagine how they might fly. Advancements in chemical know-how led to the realisation that certain gases were lighter than the air. If those lighter elements could be harnessed in some way, then flight was possible.

The original home of ballooning, and thus flight itself, was France. The key year for developing balloons was 1783. The Montgolfier brothers designed and built a balloon powered by hot air. Such was the brothers' success that they were invited to demonstrate their balloon, which carried a duck and a rooster as passengers, in front of King Louis XVI and Marie Antoinette. In late November 1783, Étienne Montgolfier made the first human flight into the sky. While the Montgolfiers were the pioneers of balloon flight, more important in the long term was the work of Professor Jacques Charles, a Parisian chemist, who had conceived of a balloon that could hold hydrogen (a more sustainable element than hot air), and therefore float into the sky. He was assisted by two engineering brothers, Anne-Jean Robert and Nicholas-Louis Robert, who were able to design and build a balloon for Professor Charles. After various tests, they launched their first balloon, named Le Globe, from the centre of Paris in August 1783. The launch was watched by a large crowd, including an elderly Benjamin Franklin. As the balloon rose, it flew northwards, and was pursued by spectators on horseback. It finally landed some 21 km away, near the village of Gonesse. Whether true or not, the story circulated that the villagers of Gonesse, who were terrified of such a strange object emerging on them from the skies, attacked the balloon with pitchforks and destroyed it. Such was the success of the experiment, that by December 1783, Professor Charles and Nicholas-Louis Robert were able to take to the air in a manned balloon for a flight of over two hours.

The craze for ballooning quickly spread beyond France, and fascinated an Irishman named Richard Crosbie. A graduate of Trinity College, Dublin,

Crosbie excelled at engineering and had been inspired by the stories from France of balloons taking to the sky. Not content with merely getting into the air, although that was his first objective, Crosbie set his sights on crossing the Irish Sea. To raise funds for his adventure, Crosbie tethered a floating balloon in Ranelagh Gardens and charged the crowds to witness his modern wonder. After testing his balloon's abilities to cross the Irish Sea, which was successfully done with a cat as passenger, Crosbie announced his intention to undertake his maiden manned flight in January 1785. Huge crowds gathered, estimated at 3,500 people and including many of the leading lights of Dublin society, paying an entrance fee to watch Crosbie launch his balloon and himself into the air. *The Annual Register* recorded how Crosbie, perhaps aware of the showmanship that such a crowd expected, wore an 'aerial dress consisted of a robe of oiled silk, lined with white fur, his waistcoat and breeches in one, of white satin quilted, and morocco boots, and a montero cap of leopard skin'. The launch was successful, and although darkness and unfavourable winds forced him to abandon his sea crossing, Crosbie was able to fly north across the city and land in Clontarf. While never making it across the Irish Sea, Crosbie's cross-Dublin flight meant he became the first Irishman to fly.

While ballooning continued to develop, there was a sense of frustration that these would always remain unpowered craft that were dependant on the elements. Thus, in the second half of the nineteenth century, inventive attention across the western world turned back to the question of how to achieve powered flight. The 1860s and 1870s witnessed various successful experiments with unpowered gliders, and it was evident that inventors were getting the basics of aerodynamics right. The real challenge for inventors was to under-stand how to power an aeroplane over distance. However, as soon as any form of power was added, the weight of the plane increased dramatically and its ability to glide severely diminished. Some pioneers, such as Gustave Whitehead, claimed to have flown a steam-powered monoplane for 3 miles across Pittsburgh in 1899, but this was never verified. It took until 1903, when the Wright brothers successfully flew their plane, the Wright Flier, that there was a verified flight of a controlled, powered and heavier-than-air machine. The aviation business had begun in earnest, and in the same way that Crosbie had quickly

Aviation advanced rapidly during the First World War, and once peace had been restored, the challenge of flying the Atlantic gave rise to intense competition. Media coverage of the various attempts was high profile, and once Alcock and Brown successfully flew the ocean, they won the £10,000 prize that had been offered by the *Daily Mail* for the first successful crossing. Despite the heroism of their feat, their landing was anything but smooth. What the airmen mistook for a smooth green field, was actually the bog on Derrygimlagh Moor and on landing the plane was seriously damaged.

This plane, the Bremen, left Dublin on 12 April 1928 to successfully complete the first east to west crossing of the Atlantic. On the plane's return to Ireland a huge crowd gathered to greet it, and days later the three pilots appeared before a celebratory crowd estimated at over 50,000 people on O'Connell Street. Here, the Bremen is readied for departure from Baldonnel.

followed the inspiration of the French balloonist, so an Irishman would be inspired by the Wright brothers to build and pilot the first Irish plane.

Harry Ferguson, from County Down, was known to those in his neighbourhood as the mad mechanic. He worked in the family garage business and was obsessed with engines. In an age when it was still unusual to even see a car, Ferguson took part in motor and motorcycle racing as a way of promoting the family business. However, racing along the ground at high speed was not enough for Ferguson. He had read about various aviation pioneers around the world, and had also travelled to the Continent to attend flying displays. He read as much as he could about flying, a passion that was fed by an increasing number of commercially available aviation magazines. In one, *Flight*, Ferguson found detailed descriptions of Louis Blériot's monoplane, in which he crossed the English Channel in July 1909, and was able to set about building his own plane. Ferguson was not alone in his enthusiasm for flight, and he was a founder member of the Irish Aero Club, which had its inaugural meeting on Dawson Street, Dublin, on 5 November 1909. The principle behind the meeting was 'that an Irish Club, to be called the Irish Aero Club, be formed, for the encouragement and support of aerial navigation'. While all members shared a common desire to fly, it was Ferguson who got airborne first. On 31 December 1909, after towing his plane behind his car from the centre of Belfast out to Hillsborough, Ferguson was able to take his monoplane into the sky. As a reporter from the *Belfast Telegraph* recorded, 'Presently, at the movement of the pedal, the aeroplane rose into the air at a height from 9 to 12 feet, amidst the heavy cheers of the onlookers. The poise of the machine was perfect and Mr Ferguson made a splendid flight of 130 yards.' Like the Wright brothers a few years earlier, the brevity of the flight did not matter. Ferguson had become the first man in Ireland to successfully build and fly a powered plane.

Ireland's pioneer was soon followed into the air by another innovator: Ireland's first woman aviator. Lillian Bland, from Carmoney, near Belfast, had been as inspired by Blériot as Ferguson, and was moved to build her own biplane. After bringing the parts in from England, Bland constructed the plane herself, and launched it into the air in 1910. After her initial successes with unpowered flight, Bland added a twenty horsepower engine, and was able to fly the biplane over a distance of a quarter of a mile. Originally hoping that her exploits would lead to a business building planes, Bland was deterred from further involvement in aviation by her father, who insisted she stop flying for her safety.

Ferguson, Bland and their fellow flight enthusiasts around the world were an elite group. They achieved something remarkable in taking their self-built planes into the skies, but flying was a hobby reserved for people of means and with a good deal of engineering knowledge. The catalyst for a rapid advancement in flight technology was the First World War, when planes were used for fighting, bombing and reconnaissance. The British Army organised its planes and pilots into a new organisation, the Royal Flying Corp (later the Royal Air Force), and during the four years of hostilities thirty-eight of the fliers were Irish-born. The four years of war, and the intense investments made in flight technology by the British and the Germans, meant that by 1918 the range, reliability and possible uses of planes had extended considerably. The great goal for many was the first crossing of the Atlantic. In 1913, a £10,000 prize was offered to the first person who could cross the Atlantic, but no one had claimed it before the outbreak of hostilities in Europe. There were many failures before, in June 1919, John Alcock and Arthur Whitten-Brown (both ex-Royal Air Force who had flown during the war) successfully flew from Newfoundland to Ireland. They flew over the west coast of Ireland, having successfully crossed the ocean, some sixteen hours after leaving Newfoundland, and landed in a bog just outside of Clifden. Not only did Alcock and Brown take the prize for the first transatlantic crossing and enter aviation history, the fact that they had landed in Ireland – the nearest European point to North America – placed the country in a prized position for the future development of commercial crossings.

In 1921, during the negotiations that would lead to the signing of the Anglo-Irish Treaty, Michael Collins took advantage of the possible benefits of flight. Worried that the British might arrest Collins if the Treaty talks broke down, a plane was purchased that was held at the ready, just outside London, to fly Collins back to Ireland if necessary. In the event, such a hasty escape was not needed, but the plane, a five-seater Martynside, became the first plane owned by the Irish Air Corps after the signing of the Treaty.

The Irish Aviation Department, as the Air Corps was originally known,

The three pilots of the Bremen who made the first east to west Atlantic crossing were Baron Von Hunefeld, the Irishman, Colonel James Fitzmaurice and Captain Koehl. Here they are photographed, shortly after the arrival back in Ireland, with Cumann na nGaedheal Taoiseach, W. T. Cosgrave.

The Air Corps played a crucial role in the development of aviation in Ireland. While many of its members dreamt of being pilots, others had to endure what they considered to be more mundane tasks. At Baldonnel, in April 1928, members of the Air Corps were put to work preparing a grass runway to ensure the safe departure of the Bremen.

was initially based at the Beggars Bush barracks. By the end of 1922, there were fourteen trained pilots in the Air Corp, and they flew regularly during the Irish Civil War of 1922–23. The main role of the Air Corp during the Irish hostilities was reconnaissance and the regular dropping of leaflets in anti-Treaty strongholds. These leaflets were aimed at encouraging anti-Treaty forces to surrender, but in all likelihood, they had little impact.

After the ending of the Civil War, the Cumann na nGaedheal government of the Irish Free State, headed by W. T. Cosgrave, began to rebuild the infrastructure of the state that had been so badly damaged by years of fighting. The government was very forward-thinking, and their most successful modernising project was the construction of the Ardnacrusha Shannon Dam and the resulting widespread electrification of Ireland. What is surprising for such a forward-thinking government was that they proved resistant to the idea of developing a national commercial airline, as many other nations were doing. In 1928, the Minister for Industry and Commerce, Patrick McGilligan, received a committee report on the potential for setting up a national airline, but the view was that such an undertaking would require substantial govern-ment investment in the early years, and was therefore too expensive. Despite their failure to envisage a national commercial airline, the first government of the state did continue to support the Air Corps, and in 1928 an Irishman played a part in one of aviation's most significant flights.

While flights across the Atlantic, flying west to east, had increased in number since Alcock and Brown's first crossing, no one had ever managed a flight east to west. Attempts had been made, but these had ended in crash landings at sea and, unfortunately, in the loss of life. The plane that would undertake the first successful east–west flight in 1928 was the German-registered Bremen. The men planning the crossing were Baron Gunther von Hunefeld and Captain Hermann Koehl. They decided to begin their attempt from Baldonnel Aerodrome in Dublin, and enlisted the help of Colonel James Fitzmaurice of the Irish Air Corp, as he had made a previous unsuccessful attempt at the crossing and knew the risks that were involved. His local knowledge and long flying experience were seen as invaluable if the flight was to succeed. The Bremen took off from Baldonnel at five o'clock in the morning, on 12 April

13

1928, and landed at Greenly Island in Canada, at six o'clock in the evening the next day. The crowds that had gathered to watch the Bremen depart were large, but they were dwarfed by the multitude that turned out when the plane landed back at Baldonnel after its historic journey. The three airmen, particularly Fitzmaurice, were feted by the Irish press and the people, and they were met by a crowd estimated at over 50,000 when they were announced at a celebratory event on O'Connell Street. The crossing of the Bremen was important for several reasons to the future of Irish aviation. It proved that the east–west crossing could be done, which meant that there was a future for commercial transatlantic travel. The crossing also demonstrated how central Ireland was to the future of aviation. As the most westerly part of Europe, Ireland was closest to North America. As such, it would always serve, until technology substantially changed, as the starting point for Atlantic crossings. Fitzmaurice believed firmly in the viability of an Irish national airline that could work both across the Irish Sea and the Atlantic. He was vociferous in his support for the idea when McGilligan's committee was gathering evidence, and astounded when the government refused to invest in a nationally operated airline. In disgust, Fitzmaurice, undoubtedly the greatest Irish aviator of his period, resigned from the Air Corp.

In the face of the absence of any coordinated attempt by the government to begin a national airline, some Irish entrepreneurs of the 1920s and early 1930s did make efforts to begin commercial flights. The first, Iona National Airways, was begun by Hugh Cahill in 1930. A motor engineer and garage owner from Dublin, Cahill was an aviation enthusiast. He purchased his first plane, a Desoutter Mark II, and began using that plane, and others he bought later, to offer flying lessons. He also sold air trips to members of the public who wanted to experience the sensation of flying, undertook aerial photography for various agencies, and was even hired to drop the match ball from a plane to mark the opening of Westmeath's GAA ground at Cusack Park, Mullingar. Cahill's most serious attempt at starting commercial operations came in October 1932. He had reached an agreement with the Dutch carrier, KLM, who were testing a Dublin to Berlin route, that he would use his plane to connect Galway with Dublin, delivering mail (and potentially passengers) for the onward KLM flight. In October 1932, the test was successfully completed,

The Air Corps would provide many of the first pilots for Aer Lingus, and their experience flying in Ireland and beyond would prove invaluable to the fledgling company. Here, at Fermoy in the 1920s, pilots from the Air Corps are seen preparing a route while their planes are made ready.

Charles Lindbergh was a giant of aviation, and a key figure in identifying the west of Ireland as an essential staging post for transatlantic flights. He carried out the surveys that led to Foynes being recognised as the perfect landing place for transatlantic sea planes. Foynes came into its own during the years of the Second World War. Here, Lindbergh, in the centre, is seen shaking hands with Eamon de Valera (on the left in aviation garb), who had flown with Lindbergh over the Foynes Estuary to watch an early transatlantic flight depart.

My Dad was a Flight Sgt in Baldonnel 1923–66. Our family lived in married quarters there until the 'Emergency' when all civilians were evacuated. Our house looked out onto the apron between two hangars, and when Aer Lingus started up in 1936, my elder brother Leo (now deceased) was very young. On many occasions, when the key to the Iolar was missing, he was hauled out of bed and would squeeze into the cockpit window, work his way through the cabin to open the door from the inside. His reward for doing so was that he was allowed to take some of the boiled sweets from the seat pockets!

Dermot Cavanan, Retired, Marketing

but despite Cahill's enthusiasm for linking Ireland with the rest of Europe, the government once more refused to support a move into the world of aviation. A year later, Hugh Cahill left the world of flying for good, and returned to his garage business. During August and September 1933, the Midland and Scottish Air Ferries company managed to run a daily service from Liverpool to Dublin, but due to poor demand, and the government's insistence that the company be registered in Ireland if it wished to continue, the service was abandoned no sooner than it had begun.

Clearly the 1920s and early 1930s had proved that there was a desire, even a need, for a commercial airline flying out of Ireland. However, until the change of government in 1932, Cumann na nGaedheal had firmly resisted the push to start up a national airline on the basis of cost. If an airline was to be founded by the state, aircraft would have to be purchased, pilots and staff hired, and ultimately a new airport built as Baldonnel was not suitable for any substantial volume of commercial traffic. It was clear that if a national airline was to be started, it would need investment from the state, and that the likely returns, in the short term at least, would be negligible.

It would be Fianna Fáil, and most importantly Seán Lemass, Minister for Industry and Commerce, who would bring a national airline into being in the 1930s. Lemass was approached in 1933 by a company calling itself the Irish Transatlantic Air Corporation, who wanted to begin a service to the

AN RÚNAIDHE.

C.A.481.

ROINN TIONNSCAIL AGUS TRÁCHTÁLA
(Department of Industry and Commerce)
Sráid Mhuirbhtheann Uacht,
(Upper Merrion Street),

BAILE ÁTHA CLIATH.

Saorstát Éireann

6 May, 1935.

Confidential.

A dhuine uasail,

I am directed by the Minister for Industry and Commerce
to inform you that he has decided to set up a small committee, with
an officer of this Department as Chairman, to advise him on the
inauguration of air transport services in the Saorstat and between
the Saorstat and other countries.

The matters for consideration by the Committee will
include:-

(1) the formation of an Air Transport Company and its
flotation - finance and scope of operation;

(2) arrangements for the operation of internal and
external services;

(3) provision of aerodromes, meteorological installations etc.

(4) provision of expert technical assistance;

(5) recruitment of staff and provision of equipment;

(6) promotion of necessary legislation.

The Minister desires me to invite you to be a member
of the Committee and I shall be glad to hear at your early
convenience whether you are willing to act.

Invitations have also been sent to:-

J.J.O'Leary,Esq.,Messrs.Cahill & Co.,Ltd.,Parkgate, Dublin.
Sean O'hUadhaigh, Solicitor, 12 Dawson Street, Dublin.
A.P.Reynolds,Esq., 57, Upper O'Connell Street, Dublin.

Mise le meas,

John Leydon

W.H.Morton, Esq.,
General Manager,
Great Southern Railways,
Kingsbridge.

United States, flying out of Galway. Nothing came out of the plan, but the prospect of commercial concerns developing flights in and out of Ireland, with no state input, galvanised Lemass and his department into action. The issue of whether the Free State would have a national airline became a regular feature in Dáil debates, and, in May 1934, Lemass announced that the question of a 'Free State Air Navigation Company' was being dealt with. In June 1934, Lemass established an interdepartmental committee to explore the options for a state-run air service between Britain and Ireland. From this came the Air Transport Committee, led by Seán Ó hUadhaigh, who would go on to be the first chairman of Aer Lingus. This committee met with Lemass in May 1935, and outlined various proposals as to how an airline could be established, and the possible routes it might use. The upshot was the presentation of the Air Navigation and Transport Bill before the Dáil and Seanad, and the creation, on 22 May 1936, of a new company, Aer Lingus Teoranta, that would be responsible for the business and pursuit of aviation in and out of the Free State.

To get Aer Lingus into the air, as the Air Navigation and Transport Bill was still working its way through the parliamentary process, the company partnered with the British firm, Blackpool and West Coast Air Services, which loaned money to Aer Lingus so that it could purchase its first plane. That first plane, a De Havilland 84 Dragon, was registered EI-ABI (EI the prefix that all Aer Lingus flights carry to this day) and given the Irish name Iolar (Eagle). The inaugural flight took place on 27 May 1936, the day after the plane had been blessed by Reverend O'Riordan, the Irish Air Corps Chaplain. It was piloted by Captain Eric Armstrong. The route was Dublin to Bristol, and departure set for 9 o'clock in the morning. Although Lemass attended

This letter, from the Department of Industry and Commerce, and addressed to W. H. Morton, the General Manager of Great Southern Railways, invites him to join the committee established to investigate the feasibility of starting an Irish, state run, air service. Morton accepted the invitation, and was a key member of the Aer Lingus Board until the late 1940s (*courtesy of the Irish Railway Record Society*).

NEW IRISH AIR SERVICE

Mass will be celebrated at Baldonnel Aerodrome this morning at 8 o'clock in connection with the inauguration of the new air services, which are to be operated jointly by Aer Lungus, Teóranta and Blackpool and West Coast Air Services, Ltd. The initial services are to be Baldonnel-Bristol and Baldonnel-Isle of Man-Liverpool.

The hours of departure are:—Baldonnel-Bristol service, from Baldonnel at 9 a.m.; arrival Bristol, 11 a.m.; departure Bristol, 12.15; arrival Baldonnel, 2.30 p.m. Dublin, Isle of Man and Liverpool service:—Departure Baldonnel, 2.15 p.m.; departure Isle of Man, 3.45 p.m.; arrival Liverpool, 4.45 p.m. Departure Liverpool, 11.30 a.m.; departure Isle of Man, 12.45 p.m.; arrival Baldonnel, 1.45 p.m. A special 'bus service to and from Baldonnel has been arranged in connection with the services.

Col. Russell, in the course of an interview with an IRISH PRESS reporter last evening, said: " To-morrow is an historic day for Ireland. We will see inaugurated the first air link between the Saorstat and the United Kingdom. The two services to be inaugurated are in the capable hands of Capt. Olley, who is a pilot of great fame, and has flown more hours than any other pilot. He is also the creator and head of the vast charter aeroplane organisation which has its home at Croydon Aerodrome, London.

" We, of the Irish aviation movement, who have struggled so long for an air link between the Saorstat and the European air system with which London is connected, wish those two services every success."

Left: The press coverage of Aer Lingus' first flight was actually quite muted, as the flight coincided with the sailing of the *Queen Mary* – the Atlantic's newest liner – that day. In this clipping from the *Irish Press*, which was a staunch supporter of the establishment of the airline, the desire that Ireland be linked to Europe, by air, is clearly stated.

Above: The Iolar is blessed the day before its maiden commercial flight to Bristol. The Chaplain of the Air Corps carried out the blessing, a tradition that would continue with all new planes accepted into the airline's fleet.

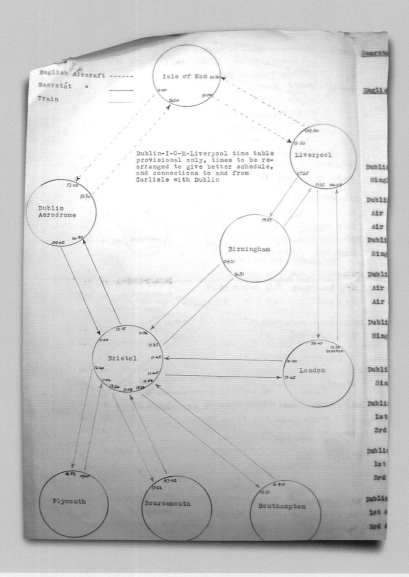

When Aer Lingus was established, there was a belief that it would rapidly expand its services to encompass the major cities of the United Kingdom. Here, in an assessment for the Department of Industry and Commerce, Aer Lingus' partner, Olley Air Services, maps out what they believed was attainable, with the departure and arrival times closely knitted together so that the most efficient use could be made of the airline's limited fleet (*courtesy of the Irish Railway Record Society*).

Baldonnel to watch the first ever Aer Lingus flight, he and other luminaries in attendance, such as Oliver St John Gogarty, did not board the plane. In fact there were only five passengers on board and the only freight was copies of *The Irish Times*. Two hours after take-off, Iolar landed in Bristol. Aer Lingus had successfully completed its maiden flight as a national airline.

While this first flight of an Aer Lingus service was hugely significant, and laid the foundation for an expansion of the company's services across Europe and North America in the decades to come, it was an event that was overshadowed in the newspapers. On the same day that Iolar took to the air, the transatlantic ship, the Queen Mary, had its maiden voyage. The newspapers were more interested in the luxury and massive capacity of the oceangoing liner, a tried and tested technology, than they were in a small plane flying a few people across the Irish Sea. Despite the ways in which flying had captured the Irish public imagination since days of Crosbie and his balloon in Ranelagh Gardens, it seemed that few could envisage a day when the esoteric technology of flight would ever replace the familiar certainty of the ship as the first transport choice for the travelling public.

By the end of 1936, Aer Lingus had added a further route to Liverpool, and had extended the Bristol flight so that it travelled onto London. The long term financial stability of the airline was underpinned in May 1937, when Aer Rianta was established under the terms of the Air Navigation and Transport Bill. This was an important step as Aer Rianta would act as the parent company for Aer Lingus, and was owned by the state. Ireland finally had in law, as well as in the form of two planes, its national airline. For Lemass the passage of the Bill, and the creation of Aer Rianta, was not only a political victory but also, to his mind, a harbinger of future potential. He argued that in time the Free State would become 'the international junction for air traffic', and that it would 'establish air services connecting the Saorstát directly with all the principal countries'. Unfortunately for the immediate future of Aer Lingus, hostilities were renewed across Europe, and the years of the Second World War saw the airline's activities reduced to a single Dublin to Liverpool service, the operation of which was frequently disrupted by safety concerns. The Lemass vision of Ireland as a transatlantic hub, and Aer Lingus as an airline flying to many of the major European cities, would have to wait.

PROPOSED ORGANISATION.

DUBLIN AIRPORT.

For the inauguration of activities at Dublin we suggest, as previously indicated, the appointment of a Station Manager to be centered at the Airport.

This gentleman's duties will comprise the controlling of all bookings, the compilation of ship's papers for internal and Customs purposes as well as correspondence in connection with traffic and general commercial matters.

He will also be responsible for the collection of fares, and the banking of monies collected, keeping in close contact with the Secretary's Office in this latter connection through a daily work record of similar type to the one attached, which will enable the Secretary to compile the Company's books.

Outside Assistant. This gentleman's principle duty will be to disburse information on the Company's activities and services to all possible sources of traffic, such as Travel Agents, Hotel and Club Porters, large Business Houses, etc., and work in close co-operation with the Station Manager with regard to weekly relief. It may be eventually considered unnecessary for this outside representative as and when the services and activities of the Company have become better known. At this time it is suggested that work at the Airport will have become far too much for one man; the representative will obviously then be primarily concerned with activities at the Airport itself.

One boy as general office boy at the Airport.

Engineer and Assistant

Left: The haste with which Aer Lingus was established meant that little thought was given to the facilities and staff needed at Baldonnel Aerodrome to service civilian flights. This letter from March 1936, from the company's Secretaries, lays out what was required at Baldonnel to ensure that everyone was checked in and boarded. The job descriptions for all the staff envisaged are fairly broad, but the addition to the staff of 'one boy' speaks more of Dickensian employment practices than that which befitted a modern airline (*courtesy of the Irish Railway Record Society*).

Above: While Aer Lingus was finally floated on the stock market in 2006 to become a public company, its establishment in 1936, although underwritten by state money, necessitated the issuing of share certificates to all members of its Board. This certificate was issued to W. H. Morton in 1936 and valued at £1 (*courtesy of the Irish Railway Record Society*).

A crowd of dignitaries gathered at Baldonnel airport to wave off the first Dublin–Bristol–London flight in 1936. Although this was a momentous event in the history of Aer Lingus, the invited crowd was not that great, and relatively few pictures survive of the day that linked Dublin with Britain's capital city.

This advertisement for Irish Sea Airways, a brand that Aer Lingus used in its early days, is from 1938. While it speaks to the desires of many tourists, that they might find the sun, it is doubtful that either Bristol or Croydon offered the respite from a typical Irish summer that its passengers were seeking.

Once they began in 1936, the Aer Lingus services across the Irish Sea became well established, but the steady growth in passenger numbers and the exploration of new routes was halted suddenly with the outbreak of war in 1939. Although Éire remained neutral, the difficulties of flying into a country at war, meant that only a Dublin – Liverpool service remained in operation until 1945. In a modern era where 70 per cent of all Aer Lingus bookings are made online, the idea of printed timetables seems old fashioned, but such documents were vital to those travel agents and passengers who were planning journeys (*courtesy of Paul Roche*).

Routes

Agadir, Barcelona, Brussels, Dubrovnik, Naples, New York, Prague and Zurich: these are just some of the current routes operated by Aer Lingus, and with connections on partner airlines, a host of other destinations worldwide are opened up. All this is a far cry from May 1936, when the inaugural flight operated by Aer Lingus was the two-hour crossing to Bristol, which carried only five passengers. In 2009, Aer Lingus carried over 10 million passengers on routes across Europe and North America. Ireland is a key airline market, and in 2009 26.3 million passengers passed through Irish airports, a multiple of 5.84 times the nation's population. Across the European Union, the multiple is an average of 1.5. For the Irish, flying is a more common experience than for any of their European counterparts, and Aer Lingus is at the heart of the flying experience. It was not always so. When W. J. Scott joined the airline as a pilot after flying in the Second World War, he referred to Aer Lingus as 'a very, very tiny airline'. From the standpoint of early 1945, this was an entirely fair comment. Aer Lingus had only three planes, and was only operating two routes. It was Scott, and all the other employees of Aer Lingus, who would oversee a rapid expansion of the airline, and its routes, in the immediate post-war years.

In November 1945, Aer Lingus reinstated its Dublin to London route, which had been suspended during the war. This reinstated route flew not from Baldonnel, as the pre-war flights had, but from the newly opened Collinstown airport. Now more commonly known as Dublin airport, Collinstown was seen as the ideal home for the city's new airport. While Aer Lingus had begun life flying out of Baldonnel, this was a military, not civilian airport, and not ideal as a permanent home for the national airline. The debates as to where the new airport should be built were rancorous, with various parties suggesting different possible locations; even Phoenix Park was held up as a contender due to its large open spaces and good transport connections to the city! Other options included a disused airfield at Cookstown, another at Kildonan, near Finglas, as well as a suggestion that Sandymount Strand be reclaimed from the sea, and the airport built on the perimeter of Dublin Bay. Ultimately the Collinstown site made the most sense from a practical and financial point of view. It sat above sea level, was mostly free of fog and the bulk of the land required was already owned by the state. The total cost of the project, from levelling the land, to building the terminal, was estimated at £360,000 – a bargain basement price compared to the hundreds of millions of euro to build the second terminal at Dublin airport in 2010. Work began on the site in 1937, and by January 1940 the Aer Lingus Dublin to Liverpool service was able to move from Baldonnel to Collinstown. The beautiful terminal building, which opened a year later, and the design by Desmond FitzGerald, reflected a different mode of travel, as it mirrored the curving bridge of an ocean liner.

An early VIP to pass through Collinstown was Wendell Lewis Willkie, who had been the Republican Party candidate in the United States Presidential election of 1940. He arrived in Collinstown from Manchester, in February 1941, following an eighty-minute flight, and after being met by Minister Frank Aitken, was driven into the city to meet Eamon de Valera in Government Buildings. *The Irish Times* reported that Willkie's drive from the airport into the city took twelve minutes, and after meetings and a luncheon, he was back in the air, and flying onto London, exactly three hours after he had first touched down. Given that the journalists who quizzed Willkie were keen to understand the United States' view of Ireland's wartime neutrality – the big issue of the day – *The Irish Times* commentary on the ease of his journey through the airport and into the city may seem an oddity. However, it was a common media theme of the time, as the construction of Collinstown was an important success story and symbol during the difficult years of the Emergency. As Clair Wills noted in *That Neutral Ireland*, the airport was part

WEST COAST AIR SERVICES LIMITED,
in Association with AER LINGUS TTA (Irish Air Lines).

TIME TABLE (WEEKDAYS ONLY).
NOVEMBER 16th 1942, UNTIL FURTHER NOTICE.
LIVERPOOL ~ DUBLIN.

			West Coast Air Services	Aer Lingus Tta
Depart	(By Coach)	Lime Street Station ...	... 09.30	13.30
Depart	(By Coach)	Adelphi Hotel ...	... 09.35	13.35
Depart	(By Air)	SPEKE AIRPORT ...	... 11.00	15.00
Arrive	(By Air)	DUBLIN AIRPORT ...	... 12.20	16.20
Arrive	(By Coach)	44 Upper O'Connell Street	... 13.05	17.05

DUBLIN ~ LIVERPOOL.

			Aer Lingus Tta	West Coast Air Services
Depart	(By Coach)	Upper O'Connell Street	... 09.15	13.45
Depart	(By Air)	DUBLIN AIRPORT ...	... 10.00	14.30
Arrive	(By Air)	SPEKE AIRPORT ...	... 11.20	15.50
Arrive	(By Coach)	Adelphi Hotel ...	... 12.15	16.50
Arrive	(By Coach)	Lime Street Station ...	... 12.20	16.55

FARES:
SINGLE: £4 RETURN (Valid 18 Days) £6 RETURN (Valid 60 Days), £7 4 0.
For Children's Fares—See Paragraph 5, Page 6.
Tickets issued by West Coast Air Services or Aer Lingus Tta, are Inter-available by the Services of either Company.
Passengers are advised in their own interests to read the "NOTES TO PASSENGERS" contained on pages 6 & 7.
BAGGAGE: Free Baggage allowed. 15 Kilos (33 lbs.)
Baggage in excess of this allowance will, subject to accommodation being available, be carried at the rate of 1/- per Kilo (2.2 lbs.)
FREIGHT & LIVESTOCK ARRANGEMENTS:
See Paragraphs 8 & 9 of "SPECIAL NOTES FOR PASSENGERS."

ROAD TRANSPORT.
Passengers are conveyed free of charge between the City and Airport Terminals shown above.

CONDITIONS OF CARRIAGE.
An extract of the conditions under which the carriage of Passengers and Baggage is undertaken, is shown on pages 2 & 3, and full conditions are displayed at the Airports served by the Company.

4   5

Wartime restrictions played heavily on Aer Lingus' ability to develop during the 1940s. Rather than further expanding its network of routes, it was restricted to a single route flying between Dublin and Liverpool. Although an unfamiliar way of travelling for many, flying proved popular during the war, as many people felt that the sea crossing between Ireland and Britain was more dangerous due to the presence of German U Boats (*courtesy of Paul Roche*).

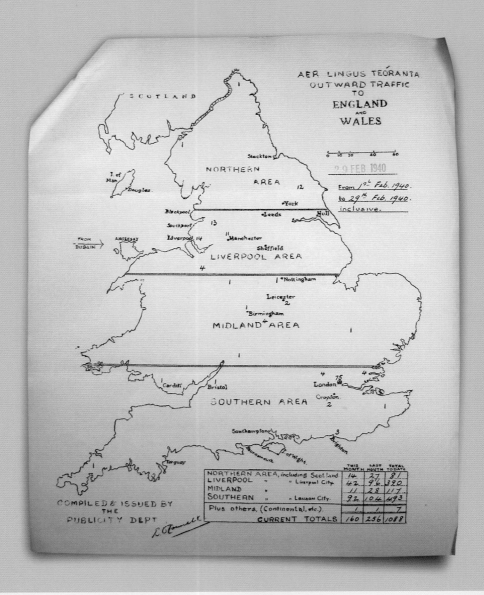

Although wartime passenger flights were restricted to the Liverpool crossing, Aer Lingus did fly various other routes to Britain during the war. These flights were mainly concerned with the movement of cargo (particularly mail) and key personnel. These maps, that were produced monthly between 1939 and 1945, show the number of total flights made (*courtesy of the Irish Railway Record Society*).

of 'Ireland's efforts to modernise, that made it part of the largest networks of communication spanning the globe'. Collinstown was not simply a new airport with a stylish terminal, but rather an embodiment of what Ireland, and in aviation terms, Aer Lingus, could achieve in the coming years. The war years and the policy of neutrality were difficult for Ireland, and hardships ensued. The airport was used more profitably until 1945 for boosting national food supplies – by growing wheat alongside the runways – than it was for flying planes. But with the ending of hostilities in 1945, Collinstown began to come into its own. Its central role in the future of Ireland was evident in the 1946 government-commissioned film *A Nation Once Again*, which was made to celebrate the life of nineteenth-century nationalist, Thomas Davis. Amongst all the historical messages of the film, there are also shots of Collinstown and the FitzGerald-designed terminal standing as 'a symbol of modern Ireland'.

With a new airport in place, and the war ended, how would Aer Lingus grow? And would there be enough paying passengers to make Aer Lingus a success? Airlines are not cheap businesses to run, and so long as flying remained the transport choice of the few who could afford it, the question remained as to where any growth in Aer Lingus' passenger base would come from.

At the end of 1945, Aer Lingus purchased five C-47 planes from the United States government. This was followed in the spring of 1946 by further purchases of DC3 planes from Pacific Northern Airlines. The successful acquisition of planes meant that the Aer Lingus fleet had grown rapidly in the months following the end of the war. What it needed now were routes and passengers. The key to growth was twofold: first, acquiring the necessary agreements to gain routes in and out of Britain, and second, to ensure that Aer Lingus had a central role in the expected growth of transatlantic services that would be centred on Shannon. The two issues came together in April 1946, when the Irish government signed an agreement with British European Airways and British Overseas Airways Corporation (BOAC), which granted the British access to Shannon, as a base for transatlantic flights, while in return Aer Lingus would have sole rights over flights between Ireland and

Britain, and would additionally be allowed to fly on from British airports to other European airports. The agreement, made into law under the 1937 Air Navigation and Transport Bill, effectively created a new company, of which 60 per cent comprised Aer Lingus and 40 per cent British European Airways and BOAC. While some commentators objected to any British involvement in Aer Lingus, pragmatically it was the wisest move. It allowed Aer Lingus unfettered access to routes across the Irish Sea at a time when the British market was vital to the economic future of the airline.

The growth of routes was instant following the agreement with the British, and in June 1946 a new Dublin to Paris route opened. This was followed in 1947 by Dublin to Amsterdam via Manchester; Dublin to Brussels; Dublin to Glasgow via Manchester; Shannon to London; Shannon to Paris via Dublin; Dublin to Liverpool via Belfast; and Dublin to Rome. While this was all good news, and the sign of a growing company, insiders at Aer Lingus, such as the future Taoiseach Garrett FitzGerald, who was in charge of market planning and scheduling from 1947 to 1958, felt such rapid expansion was premature. Put simply, where were the passengers? The Shannon route to Paris was a case in point. The logic behind the route was that it would link with a transatlantic flight operated by an American airline, and the passengers from that flight would journey onto Paris on board Aer Lingus. That transatlantic flight never materialised, and the only potential passengers were those needing to travel from the Shannon area. As a result, the route attracted no fare-paying passengers in the second half of October 1947, a bare two weeks after it had opened. The story was little different across many of the other routes that had been opened with such enthusiasm in the summer of 1947.

One of the key sites in the Aer Lingus story, Shannon airport flourished in the decades after the Second World War. Although Aer Lingus did not fly over the Atlantic until 1958, it had used the airport from its inception to fly transatlantic passengers onto other Europe wide destinations. The airport was open twenty-four hours a day, and overworked staff had to grab a rest anywhere, and anytime, they could (*courtesy of Kay O'Rourke*).

The central logic behind many of the routes was the development of a transatlantic service by Aer Lingus. In this, Shannon was the key. The early transatlantic aviators, from Alcock and Brown onwards, had shown how important Ireland was to transatlantic flight. Ireland was the nearest landmass to North America, and the quickest place to get to. This logic had benefitted Foynes during the war years, when it was used as the landing place for the seaplanes that crossed the Atlantic. Seaplanes, by 1945, were not, despite their obvious glamour, the future. The rapid development of aviation technology during the war years meant that land planes would be the next phase in transatlantic flight. The Irish had anticipated this, and while Foynes flourished during the war, work began on a new facility at Rineanna, that would eventually be known as Shannon airport, as early as 1937. By the end of the war, Shannon had four concrete runways, the longest of which stretched to 10,000 feet, and were able to accommodate the most modern planes. Almost immediately, Shannon became the single most important airport for long haul flights, accepting airlines from across the United States and Europe as they used the location as a staging post for flights to and from North America. The appeal of Shannon was enhanced in 1947, when it became the world's first Customs Free Area. Outside the airport this led to a boom as industrial units relocated to Shannon, and were able to avoid import and export taxes; inside the airport it led to the creation of Duty

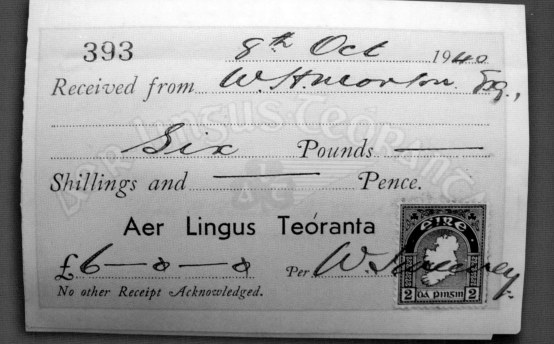

393   8ᵗʰ Oct   1940

Received from *W. H. Neorson Esq.,*

Six Pounds ————

Shillings and ———— Pence.

Aer Lingus Teóranta

£6 — 8 — 8   Per *W. Sweeney*

No other Receipt Acknowledged.

For each ticket that was bought for an Aer Lingus flight, until carbon papered tickets became the norm in the 1950s, a handwritten receipt was given. This receipt from 1940, to cover the cost of a return flight to Liverpool, offers an excellent illustration of how the airline's logo had become a standard presence on all its paperwork in a short space of time (*courtesy of the Irish Railway Record Society*).

EIRE.

TREATY SERIES, 1937

No. 3.

EXCHANGE OF NOTES

BETWEEN THE

Government of Saorstát Eireann

AND THE

American Government

IN REGARD TO

Air Navigation

Dublin, September 29/November 4, 1937.

PRESENTED TO DÁIL EIREANN BY THE MINISTER
FOR EXTERNAL AFFAIRS.

DUBLIN:
PUBLISHED BY THE STATIONERY OFFICE.

To be purchased directly from the
GOVERNMENT PUBLICATIONS SALE OFFICE, 3-4 COLLEGE ST., DUBLIN,
or through any Bookseller.

Price Twopence.

(P. No. 2939.)

Free Shops for all passengers on international journeys. The issue for Aer Lingus was whether it could organise itself, and the necessary funds, to play a role in the booming transatlantic traffic that was flying in and out of its own backyard.

To facilitate the potential transatlantic route, the government established a new company, Aerlinte Éireann, which would oversee the business of flying the Atlantic. Through Aerlinte, offices were opened in New York and Boston to promote the envisaged Aer Lingus routes from Shannon to those cities. The inaugural flight was set for 1948, and in preparation five new Constellation planes were ordered. Such was the excitement surrounding the transatlantic route, that when the first two Constellation planes, the St Brendan and the St Patrick, were flown into Dublin airport for delivery to Aer Lingus, over 12,000 people turned out to catch a glimpse of the future of Irish aviation. In February 1948, just months before the inaugural flight was due to depart, Fianna Fáil failed to win enough seats in a snap general election that it had called, and was out of government. Aer Lingus lost its most strident political supporter, as Seán Lemass would no longer be the minister responsible for aviation. The new coalition government, which was facing a torrent of financial problems, took a bleak view of the Aer Lingus accounts. In the year prior to the election it had trading losses of over £800,000, and while the transatlantic route was a bold initiative, the new government was not convinced of its viability. The move into transatlantic travel was cancelled, the new Constellation planes sold off, and the Shannon to Paris, Dublin to Rome, Dublin to Belfast and Dublin to Brussels routes, as well as the Dublin to London cargo service,

Barely a year after Aer Lingus had flown its first commercial flight, the Irish government entered into negotiations with its United States counterpart to agree the ground rules for how any future transatlantic routes might work. Ireland's geographical position gave it great strength in such governmental debates. The 1937 Notes, that were put before the Dáil that year, secured the position of Shannon as the entry and exit point for all transatlantic traffic (*courtesy of the Irish Railway Record Society*).

were all mothballed. Rather than building on the immediate post-war expansion, Aer Lingus was reducing in size. Over 250 staff were laid off, and the offices in New York, Boston and London closed. While the coalition government sought to balance the books, Aer Lingus shrunk, and other international airlines took advantage of one less competitor on the transatlantic route.

In the absence of a North American adventure, Aer Lingus concentrated on routes across the Irish Sea. London was a key route, and such was its popularity, night flights, named Starflights, were introduced. In an innovative move, Aer Lingus also began developing different price structures for tickets, and offered cheap single fares to London ranging from £4 midweek to £5 at weekends. As Garrett FitzGerald noted, 'we are really competing with surface transport at its own fare level'. This was an important development. Whereas early flights had been a choice of luxury, now Aer Lingus was competing with the ferry and rail companies, and flying to London became the option for many. By the end of 1957, just shy of a decade since the cutbacks of 1948, Aer Lingus was flying ten routes across the Irish Sea, and had carried 411,966 paying customers in a single year.

The stability in the Irish–British routes was further underpinned in 1956, when the post-war deal between Aer Lingus, British European Airways and BOAC was renegotiated. This reduced the British holding in Aer Lingus to 10 per cent, and gave the airline the right to develop European routes out of Manchester airport. This would, by the early 1960s, allow for the development of Manchester as a European hub for Aer Lingus, with regular flights to Copenhagen, Dusseldorf, Zurich, Frankfurt and Amsterdam.

By the end of the 1950s, transatlantic flights had become an everyday occurrence. Pan Am, TWA, KLM, Sabena, Air France and BOAC were all flying the Shannon to the United States route profitably, and the airport was operating twenty-four hours a day. While Aer Lingus benefited in flying transatlantic customers onwards from Shannon to other destinations in Europe, they were still not flying west across the Atlantic. However, with the victory of Fianna Fáil in the 1951 general election, and the return of Lemass to the Department of Industry and Commerce, the transatlantic issue was reignited. Not only were passenger numbers through Shannon very good – 200,882 in 1953 – but

With an increased number of routes by the early 1950s, and the associated need to attract paying passengers, Aer Lingus began to become far more visually aware of its image. This 1951 timetable stresses the shamrock identity of the airline, the modernity of its planes and, in the background, the curving lines of Dublin airport.

THE "FREEDOMS" OF THE AIR.

CHART RELATED TO A HYPOTHETICAL AEROPLANE BELONGING TO NATION "A".

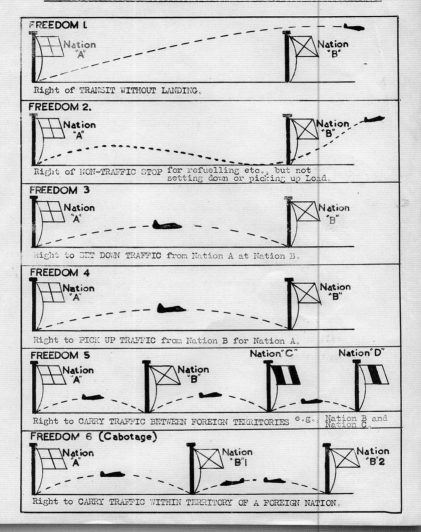

FREEDOM 1

Nation "A"   Nation "B"

Right of TRANSIT WITHOUT LANDING.

FREEDOM 2.

Nation "A"   Nation "B"

Right of NON-TRAFFIC STOP for refuelling etc., but not setting down or picking up Load.

FREEDOM 3

Nation "A"   Nation "B"

Right to SET DOWN TRAFFIC from Nation A at Nation B.

FREEDOM 4

Nation "A"   Nation "B"

Right to PICK UP TRAFFIC from Nation B for Nation A.

FREEDOM 5

Nation "A"   Nation "B"   Nation "C"   Nation "D"

Right to CARRY TRAFFIC BETWEEN FOREIGN TERRITORIES e.g. Nation B and Nation C

FREEDOM 6 (Cabotage)

Nation "A"   Nation "B" 1   Nation "B" 2

Right to CARRY TRAFFIC WITHIN TERRITORY OF A FOREIGN NATION.

Left: Until the advent of open skies policies at the end of the twentieth century, airlines could not simply choose where they flew to. Access to different nations and airports was strictly controlled by a process of freedoms, which dictated what function an airline could perform in any given country. Freedoms were a complex issue, and new to many of the airline's new post-war staff. *Aer Scéala*, the company's magazine for employees, took the opportunity in March 1948 to illustrate what the different freedoms meant to Aer Lingus.

Above: The postwar expansion of Aer Lingus' routes was signalled by the scheduling of flights to many major European cities. Taken on the runway at Rome in 1947, this crew flew one of the last proving flights before the passenger service began. The Constellation was flown by Captain I. B. Hammond, but the crew also included a feature of 1940s and 1950s flying, the navigator, radio operator and flight engineer.

the decision by the government that year to stage the first An Tóstal Festival (Ireland at Home), as a way of encouraging tourists and Irish emigrants to visit Ireland during the spring, meant that passenger numbers would be boosted. Indeed, the original idea for An Tóstal had come from Pan Am, who were searching for a way of increasing transatlantic passenger numbers outside of the busy summer season. In 1952, Lemass put in place an agreement with a United States airline, Seaboard and Western, to lease suitable transatlantic planes from them, until such time that Aer Lingus could purchase their own. In the event, administrative complications from the United States Aeronautics Board, and another change of government in Ireland, in 1954, again delayed the plans.

By 1957, Fianna Fáil were once more in government, and Lemass again pushed the transatlantic link as being vital to the future of Aer Lingus and the economic well-being of the nation. This time the dream was made real. On 28 April 1958, a leased Super-Constellation, the St Patrick, flew from Dublin to Shannon, and shortly after midnight, onwards to Boston and New York. A blizzard forced the re-routing of the plane to Nova Scotia, and arrival in New York was a day late. Despite the delay, the arrival of the first transatlantic Aer Lingus flight was seen as momentous, and it was greeted by a raft of Irish, Irish-American and international dignitaries, and a blaze of press attention. Although there were criticisms over the quality of the Aer Lingus sales operation in the United States, the first year of the transatlantic service was seen as a success, having carried 14,781 passengers, comfortably above the initial forecast of 13,000. By 1960, Aer Lingus finally took ownership of its own transatlantic planes, and ended its lease deal with Seaboard and Western.

In the late 1940s, despite having a relatively small staff, Aer Lingus began publishing *Aer Scéala* for its employees. In addition to features on the social and sporting lives of the airline's workers, the magazine also afforded Aer Lingus an important opportunity to impart information regarding business performance. Taken from the July 1959 issue, this chart illustrates how different routes were performing and the passenger revenues brought in.

ROUTE ANALYSIS OF AER LINGUS PASSENGER REVENUE

		Passenger Revenue (excl. Charters)	% of Total
	LONDON	£1,141,517	41·4%
	ENGLAND/WALES & JERSEY	£641,797	23·1%
	SCOTLAND/ ISLE OF MAN	£226,252	8·2%
	PARIS	£127,171	4·6%
	CONTINENT VIA MANCHESTER	£265,610	9·6%
	CONTINENT VIA LOURDES	£328,824	11·9%
	SHANNON	£34,605	1·2%
	TOTAL	**£2,765,776**	**100%**

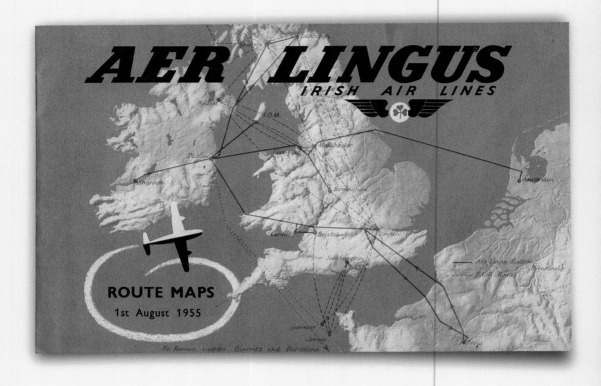

AER LINGUS

IRISH AIR LINES

ROUTE MAPS

1st August 1955

Although on board magazines would not emerge until the late 1960s, booklets of route maps were supplied to Aer Lingus passengers from the 1950s. These clearly depicted the main routes that the airline flew to Britain and on into Europe, and were rich in detail. Not simply was it enough to know where you were flying, but also what you were flying over and the location of the radar stations that were guiding the pilot.

These new planes were built by Boeing, and were B720s: the first purchase of a jet engine plane by the airline, and the ones that would carry the shamrock logo across the Atlantic. The modernity of Aer Lingus' new planes, and the visibility of an Irish livery on planes at New York and Boston airports, was hugely significant. No longer was Ireland, in the form of Shannon, a staging post between North America and Europe. Rather it was home to an Irish international airline that would build its reputation on its schedule, safety, service and friendliness. In effect, Aer Lingus embodied Ireland in the air.

The growth of Aer Lingus routes across Europe increased following the successful launch of the transatlantic service. A significant route opening came in 1954, when the airline began a service to the pilgrimage site of Lourdes, via Dinard. Catholic Ireland had a tradition of pilgrimage, and the opening of Lourdes by air from Dublin proved highly popular. Such was demand that in 1958, a specific building, the Lourdes terminal, was constructed to expedite pilgrimage passengers through Dublin airport. Not just Lourdes, but France in general was seen as a key destination for Aer Lingus in the late 1950s and early 1960s, catering for both business and tourist customers. The Biarritz route was opened in 1955, Cherbourg in 1960, and Rennes via Jersey in 1961. In time, Lourdes became an important hub for Aer Lingus, through which most flights to southern Europe would pass.

As air travel became ever more efficient into the 1960s, and also more affordable, so the opportunities grew. These days we are used to an airline map of Ireland, indeed the world, which embraces smaller regional airports. The opening of Cork airport in October 1961, something that had long been demanded by the city, was the first such regional airport in Ireland, and an opening that was seen by many as a risky undertaking. In the event, Aer Lingus fully embraced the new airport, and began flights to Dublin (despite objections from the rail company CIE, who feared a loss of custom), Bristol, Cardiff and London, later adding Barcelona, Birmingham, Jersey, Lourdes and Paris.

Aer Lingus had always taken an all-Ireland view of airline traffic, using Belfast airport for different routes over the years. In 1960 it opened an office in the city, and in 1968 began a Belfast to New York service via Shannon. The

A shot of the inaugural Dublin–Shannon–New York flight, taken from the airport balcony, in 1958. The Super Constellation, the St Patrick, and the very idea of Aer Lingus crossing the Atlantic, was a source of great fascination and a good deal of press coverage.

Each of the major inaugural flights were recorded by press photographers, as well as by the airline. In October 1958, Nuala Walsh, Ros McCarthy and Bride Gilheony prepare to welcome passengers on board the inaugural Dublin–Shannon–Boston flight.

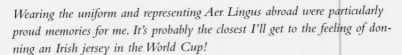

Wearing the uniform and representing Aer Lingus abroad were particularly proud memories for me. It's probably the closest I'll get to the feeling of donning an Irish jersey in the World Cup!

Margaret Brown, Retired, Travel Shop

timing was unfortunate. As the new route began, the Northern Troubles flared up, and the sight of violence on the streets, British Army involvement and paramilitary bombings became common viewing on television screens across the world. The Troubles did not simply bring into question the Belfast route, but severely damaged Ireland's reputation across the world and would have a negative impact on Aer Lingus' passenger numbers. By 1971, the ferocity of the Troubles led insurers to demand that Aer Lingus and Aerlinte pay a special war risk insurance that cost them over £500,000. The negative connotations the world was associating with Ireland and things Irish saw a steep fall in passengers, especially on transatlantic routes, and a yearly loss for 1971–72 of £2.3 million.

One answer to the airlines problems was to diversify. In the early 1970s it invested in the Tara Hotel in London, a golf course in Surrey and a hotel complex in Tenerife: all aimed at building on the increasing amount of time, and money, that the public was committing to leisure, travel and holidays. This was followed by moves into the financial services and computing sectors that would pay rich financial rewards, and in terms of the passenger experience, would lead to Aer Lingus having one of the earliest computerised booking and seat allocation systems in the aviation industry.

Despite the success of the diversification of the business, detailed in a later chapter, routes and passenger numbers remained the core concern. The Troubles continued to impact on bookings, with American and British tourists

With comparatively little security, and far fewer passengers circulating through the airport, checking in for flights in the late 1950s was a far more leisurely pursuit than many people find it now. Here passengers check in at the Aer Lingus desk at Dublin airport for an early transatlantic flight.

increasingly nervous of travelling to what the media portrayed as a war zone, without necessarily distinguishing the troubled streets of Belfast, Derry and elsewhere from the Irish Republic. By 1979, Aer Lingus closed down its Montreal route (which had run since 1966), and a year later the equally unprofitable Chicago service was also ended. However, across the European routes there were positive developments, such as the opening of Spain as a tourist destination for the Irish and the success of Aer Lingus' Aer Tours brand. But there were also negatives. In 1978, the British authorities ended the airline's favoured status at Manchester airport, and routes through there to Belgium, Germany, Holland and Scandinavia were ended.

The lack of a British hub had a detrimental effect on Aer Lingus in the short term. Effectively, it was restricted to flying to and from Ireland, and could not operate onward flights through other European cities. In the 1980s a number of smaller cities began opening airports, and Aer Lingus invested in commuter planes that could take advantage of new routes to Liverpool and Leeds/Bradford. The collapse of an independent Irish airline, Avair, in 1984, benefitted Aer Lingus as it was given permission to fly from Dublin to East Midlands, as well as to operate a greater number of commuter planes from Cork and Shannon to Dublin. Later in the 1980s, routes to Galway and Sligo, and across the Irish Sea to Newcastle and Stansted, were also opened.

In the last decades of the twentieth century, external forces changed the European airline business forever. The European Union decreed in 1985 that the dominant system across the continent, of national airlines, was detrimental to the interests of competition in the airline business and ultimately to the customer. A new era in European aviation was born under the terms of the open skies policy. One of the largest and most successful beneficiaries of the

Aer Lingus was successful in selling itself as a key carrier across the Atlantic, and not simply from Irish destinations. By using its other routes through Britain and Europe, Aer Lingus was able to connect passengers to onward transatlantic flights, such as with the Manchester to New York connection advertised in the late 1950s.

MANCHESTER - NEW-YORK

fly
IRISH AIR LINES

AER LINGUS ✱ AERLINTE EIREANN

Flying to North America, from the late 1950s and into the early 1960s, usually required a fuelling stop in Gander, on the north-eastern tip of Newfoundland. While the nearest commercial airport on the route from Ireland, Gander was notorious for its winter weather, with January average temperatures of -11°C. This scene, from 1961, would be familiar to all who broke their journey in Gander, until the stop became obsolete in the late 1960s.

AER LINGUS · IRISH

Timetable Summer 1967
Effective from May 1-October 31

Am-chlár Samhradh 1967
I bhfeidhm ó 1ú Bealtaine go dtí 31ú Deireadh Fomhair

Timetables for Aer Lingus flights were a common sight through to the 1990s. Most bookings were either made in Aer Lingus travel shops, based in the major cities from which the airline flew, or else through a travel agent. Prior to the advent of computerised booking in 1969, the printed timetable offered the most up to date information about routes and timings.

change in aviation business practice was Ryanair, founded by former Aer Lingus employee, Tony Ryan. Now the largest airline in Europe, Ryanair changed the ways in which airlines functioned. 'No frills' was the catchphrase, and their success in terms of passenger numbers saw the emergence of other low fare airlines such as Easyjet. The question for established national airlines, like Aer Lingus, especially as Ryanair was operating from an Irish base, was how to meet the challenge? Should Aer Lingus stand aloof, and operate as a traditional national airline, or should it reconfigure itself as a budget airline?

At the end of the 1980s, despite the challenges from the putative Ryanair, Aer Lingus was expanding its routes. The dispute with the British over Aer Lingus flights operating from their airports was resolved, and new routes established onwards from Birmingham and Manchester. Overall, Aer Lingus recorded a profit of £41.3 million in 1989. In 1990 the airline was granted what it had long wanted, a route to the west coast of the United States, but because of problems within the airline, the Los Angeles route did not begin as scheduled in 1991. The 1990s were a torrid time for international air travel. The Gulf War, ongoing political instability in the Middle East, an economic downturn and rising fuel costs all hit the aviation industry hard. Aer Lingus was not immune to the problems, and the very survival of the airline was in doubt during the early 1990s. After a period of intense cutbacks and redundancies, which were resisted by the various trade unions involved, Aer Lingus was able to balance its books and survive. The attacks on New York and Washington on 11 September 2001, and the ensuing wars in Iraq and Afghanistan, further destabilised the international aviation industry, and Aer Lingus' passenger numbers on its transatlantic routes were again badly hit, and many feared for the future of the airline.

Despite the broader problems in international travel, the rise of budget airlines and the need for restructuring in Aer Lingus, the late 1990s and early 2000s witnessed the rise of the Celtic Tiger. Aer Lingus benefitted from the greater wealth within Ireland, and from external interest in the country. The decision was made to float the airline on the Dublin and London stock markets. During these years Aer Lingus' conception of European routes changed utterly. No longer was there a need to concentrate solely on daily flights to

The Northern troubles had a devastating impact on Aer Lingus passenger numbers, particularly from the United States. While no laughing matter, *Mad* magazine used the high profile of Northern Ireland's conflict as the backdrop to this cartoon, which perhaps made some tourists think twice about flying.

major cities, but rather there could be a fluid model of how Ireland connected to the regions of the European Union. Flights began operating two or three times a week to tourist destinations such as Malaga and the Black Sea, to new areas of Irish business and investment including Bulgaria, and to various eastern European cities that connected the new Irish population, such as the Poles and the Latvians, with home. This European growth coincided with a growth of long haul routes offered by the airline, with destinations such as Dubai (2006–08), Los Angeles, Orlando, San Francisco (2007–09) and Washington being added. The new American routes were a product of the adoption by the United States of an open skies policy, and Aer Lingus was the first European airline to take advantage of the newly available access to American routes. Aer Lingus had chosen to meet the challenges of the industry by operating similarly to a budget airline across Europe, but in the manner of a two-class, full service airline on its international routes. Shortly after flotation, Aer Lingus left the One World alliance, which it had been involved with since 1999, and instead concentrated on code-share alliances with British Airways, KLM and United, and a United States-based partnership with Jet Blue, that allows Aer Lingus passengers to connect with flights to all major North American cities. Since 2007, Aer Lingus has run a base at Belfast International, and serves eleven different European destinations, including the important Belfast to Heathrow route. Additionally, a London base was established at Gatwick, and serves Dublin, Knock, Malaga and Cork. In 2010, Aer Lingus announced an agreement with Aer Arann, an Irish regional airline, to establish a new joint service within Ireland under the name Aer Lingus Regional. In 2010, Aer Lingus became the first airline to operate to the United States via a third party nation, when it inaugurated its Madrid to Washington service.

As it enters its seventy-fifth year, Aer Lingus exists as a private-listed company. It employs 3,500 people, and in 2009 had revenues of €1.2 billion, having flown 10 million passengers. Its two biggest shareholders are its rival, Ryanair, and the Irish government, and yet despite its flotation, it is still viewed at home and abroad as Ireland's national airline. The shamrock logo on the fleet's tailfins is a recognisable sight at the sixty-plus European, and five United States destinations that Aer Lingus flies into. Its route map, which began with a single line drawn across the Irish Sea, from Dublin to Bristol, now looks like a complex spiderweb, stretching across Ireland, into Europe and onwards to North America.

3 Planes

Driving down the side road of Dublin airport, which borders the main runway, there is always a small crowd to be witnessed. It is the same at airports across the world. The crowd, mostly male, it has to be said, stand and watch the planes come and go, but for them, this is not a passive activity. These people know their planes. They are collecting details and data, recognising plane and manufacture types, noting the livery and origin of each arrival, taking photographs and recording engine noises. These are the real fans of aviation, the knowledgeable ones. For most of us, boarding a plane is an acquiescent experience. We are more interested in where we are going, or perhaps which movies are on offer, than the vehicle we are sitting in. It is a plane that will get us safely and speedily from A to B, and that is all we need to know. And yet we should know, and pay a little more attention. All these planes we fly on, whether a short hop across Ireland, a flight to the Continent or long haul to the United States, are all different, and products of aeronautical research and design stretching across the decades and the airlines understanding of how best to get us, comfortably and efficiently, where we want to go. For airlines such as Aer Lingus, the purchase of a plane is a big undertaking (like the investment in the family car, but on a much larger scale), and it has to fit its purpose. As routes and passenger numbers shift, technology and designs change, or simply with the passage of time, planes have to replaced, and the process of selecting the new fleet begins again. This process of purchase and replacement has been a constant feature of Aer Lingus' history as the aviation industry, and the demands of the customer, never stand still. From the six-seater De Havilland 84 Dragon – the Iolar of 1936 – through to the ultra-modern

Airbus A350 XWB, due for delivery in 2015, Aer Lingus has been in a constant process of buying, selling, leasing and repairing its fleet.

Aer Lingus' first plane was sourced from Captain Gordon Olley, of Olley Air Services. The De Havilland that Olley offered to the new airline had originally been purchased by him for £2,900. In the context of 1936 it was a modern plane, with a top speed of 120 mph. To our modern eyes, the Iolar seems incredibly small, more the type of plane a flying enthusiast might own, rather than the flagship of a commercial airline. Beyond its six seats, the Iolar had room for a toilet and space for the pilot in the cockpit. The skill of the pilot in those days cannot be understated. This was years before air traffic control stations, satellite guidance systems and clear air-to-ground communication, and Captain Armstrong, on that inaugural flight, had to operate with a radio that could transmit, but not receive messages. The Iolar was sold by Aer Lingus in 1938, back to Olley Air Services, but sadly shot down into the sea by the Luftwaffe in 1941. A question for Aer Lingus, once established, was how to move forward? Clearly a six-seater aircraft was not going to establish a national airline, nor in the long term be economically viable. As Edward MacSweeney wrote to *The Irish Times,* on 20 June 1936, a month after the Bristol service had been inaugurated, the services 'have been but poorly advertised, and the Irish traveller will need a good deal of educating up to the idea of using them'. Herein lay the difficulty for Aer Lingus. As much as flying had become an item of interest and fascination for the public, the idea that they themselves might avail of commercial air services in large numbers was, for most, inconceivable. Whether it was the impression that flying was expensive, or simply that not many people wanted to travel from Dublin to Bristol by air, Aer Lingus had to expand its fleet and its capacity quickly if it was going to grow its business.

The move to expansion came quickly, with the airline taking ownership of a De Havilland DH 86A, named Éire, in September 1936. This was put on the Bristol route, which was expanded onwards to London, while Iolar was reassigned to the new Dublin to Liverpool service. A crossing through to London was seen as hugely important to the growth of the airline. In the days before the launch of the service, the newspapers were full of excitement of

Bought for just under £3,000, the Iolar, a De Havilland 84 Dragon, was Aer Lingus' first ever plane. Although the original was destroyed during the Second World War, a similar Dragon was reconditioned and flown as part of the airline's 50th anniversary in 1986.

what this meant for Irish travellers: 'the Continent of Europe will be brought, for the first time, within easy reach of Dublin. The passenger who starts at Baldonnel in the morning can enjoy luncheon – admittedly a somewhat belated luncheon – in Paris or Brussels, tea in Amsterdam, or dinner in Berlin or Copenhagen.' How many passengers rushed to avail of Continental dining is not clear, but in the years before the outbreak of the Second World War, passenger numbers grew, especially on the London route, and again the airline stepped into the market to acquire a new plane. In February 1938, Aer Lingus bought a De Havilland Rapide, which was given the name Iolar II on the retirement of the original. It was faster than any plane the airline owned, with a cruising speed of 135 mph, and most importantly it offered, as *The Irish Times* reported on 22 February 1938, increased 'seating accommodation on the London route for rush occasions. The capacity of the large Éire has been taxed recently.'

The growth in air travel was stunted during the war, but as no one knew how long hostilities would last, Aer Lingus did, during 1939 and 1940, acquire newer, faster and most importantly, bigger planes. The need to upgrade the fleet was driven by the rise in passenger numbers, prior to 1940, and the fact that the new Collinstown airport, with its larger runways, was due to come on stream. The first plane to fly out of Collinstown was a Lockheed 14 W-F62. In December 1939, the government had decided to allow Aer Lingus to proceed with its next purchase, two Douglas DC-3 planes. The first plane was shipped from the Douglas factory in Long Beach, California to Antwerp by sea, and then reassembled by Fokker workers. It was then moved to Brussels, from where Aer Lingus were due to collect and fly their new plane home. This would have all been routine, but for the fact that the German Army was ready to invade Belgium. On 10 May 1940, the day that Aer Lingus' Captain Blythe flew the plane from Brussels to Dublin, via London, the Blitzkrieg of German forces began. The speed of the Germans, in moving on Belgium, meant Aer Lingus could have well lost its plane. More pointedly, the exercise showed how fragile commercial aviation conditions were going to be during a protracted war. Given the impossibility of shipping the second DC-3 across the Atlantic, the decision was made not to proceed with the purchase, and it

I loved the whole thing of flying. In the 1960s not too many people were 'seasoned' travellers, and many needed reassurance. Many older people would be going to holiday with their children who had emigrated to England, and would be terrified if there was much turbulence. The Viscounts were turbo-prop engines so never flew higher than about 15,000 feet, so there were times when it was a bit rough. Many who travelled to and from England were either seeking jobs or coming back for funerals of loved ones, especially the 'starlight' and 'dawn' Heathrow flights.

Kay O'Rourke, Retired, Cabin Operations

was sold to Pan Am. The DC-3 that had been flown from Belgium was put into service on the Dublin to Liverpool wartime route on 17 May 1940. A sign of how things had progressed in the four years since the Iolar had first flown, was evidenced by the capacity of the DC-3 being over three times greater, at twenty-one seats available, and the cost of purchase being ten times greater at £30,000. As wartime flying conditions across the Irish Sea were highly restrictive, Aer Lingus used the DC-3 for pleasure flights, so that people could experience flight for the first time. These flights, which were regularly sold out, took passengers on a route from Collinstown across to Shannon, where it landed so passengers could enjoy lunch, and then onwards up the west coast as far as the Aran Islands, and then back to Dublin. While these flights may have only slightly boosted the airlines coffers, they gave the public a chance to familiarise themselves with flying, and perhaps won over many future customers for the post-war period.

After the war, and with the expansion of Aer Lingus routes across the Irish Sea, the airline bought a number of Douglas DC-3s in 1946. Sourcing aircraft after the war was far from easy. Aircraft production had to be switched in the United States and Britain from fighter and bomber planes back to commercial aircraft, and what was made during the early post-war years was earmarked

During the Second World War, Aer Lingus' planes were camouflaged to make them less conspicuous while in the sky. Despite wartime restrictions on flying, planes still had to be regularly maintained, and all of that work took place in hangar number one, at Dublin airport.

for the larger United States carriers who committed themselves to bulk orders. For small airlines such as Aer Lingus, sourcing aircraft was tough, and relied on ingenuity. In the event, the airline took the Douglas DC-3s from the US Army, which had been using them as troop carriers. These were flown to Scotland for conversion from the United States and Germany, and once operational from the spring of 1946, passengers would have not known that their 'new' plane had, but a few weeks before, possessed a gun turret and a full arsenal of weapons. Fortunately, by the autumn of 1946, Aer Lingus was able to announce that it had ordered seven brand new Vickers Vikings for use on its British and European routes. At a cost of £50,000 each, the planes could carry twenty-four passengers each. Most significantly, they reduced the flying time from Dublin to London to ninety minutes, and they could carry larger weights of freight. These planes were delivered and registered from June 1947, and flew a variety routes for barely a year, before being sold on. They were expensive to run, pilots did not like them, and the routes that they had been bought for proved uneconomical. As one newspaper editorial commented in January 1948, given the expected loss for the taxpayer on selling the aircraft, 'the taxpayer may have no right to choose the shoe, but he should at least be able to be told where it is pinching'. The only significant legacy of the Vickers Vikings was that they were the beginning of the tradition of naming all new Aer Lingus planes after a saint. At the end of the war, and the resumption of normal service, various minds at Aer Lingus had turned their attention as to how best planes could be labelled so as to project an Irish image to the world. In 1946, after a list of bird names had been rejected, the

St Aidan, at Dublin airport in the 1950s, sports the shamrock livery of Aer Lingus. Departing from the beautifully curved runway side of Desmond FitzGerald's terminal building, St Aidan, like all propeller planes, required some human intervention to get things moving.

The Lockheed Constellations are readied for delivery to Aer Lingus at Burbank in California in 1947. Although the planes were flown to Ireland in September 1947, led by the St Patrick in the foreground, they were never flown on their intended transatlantic route. Instead they became the workhorses of the Dublin to London route, before being sold on.

decision was made to christen all Aer Lingus planes after a saint. In July 1947, the first blessing of the fleet took place at Dublin airport. The ceremony was performed by the Reverend W. Kenry of Swords, and in front of Jimmy O'Brien, the Director of Aer Lingus, and other dignitaries, the planes, St Malachy (a DC3) and St Ronan (a Viking), were blessed, as were, in absentia, the other eighteen aircraft belonging to the company. After the blessing, Reverend Kenry, the other clergy in attendance, the dignitaries and members of the press were taken on a flight over Dublin Bay on board the St Ronan. The tradition of blessing the fleet became an annual spectacle for the airline, and to this day all new aircraft purchased by Aer Lingus are named after a saint.

The largest, and to that date, single most expensive purchase Aer Lingus made, was an order for five Constellations, to be built by the Lockheed company, at a cost of £250,000 each. In addition, £45,000 would also be spent to send staff over to the United States so they could be trained in how to fly and maintain the planes. The planes could carry fifty-eight passengers each, and were bought specifically for a transatlantic route. After delivery, in September 1947, they were pressed into service on the Dublin to London route, and also employed on the new Dublin to Rome service. This had been inaugurated in November 1947, and waved off by Taoiseach Eamon de Valera, and its first passengers had included the ever supportive Seán Lemass. However, the Constellations were expensive to run on European routes, and were not attracting the necessary passenger numbers. With the decision to postpone the move of Aer Lingus into the transatlantic market in 1948, the planes, by June that year, had been sold off.

In the years following the decision to delay the transatlantic services, and the curtailment of many European routes, Aer Lingus concentrated on buying small numbers of planes with proven efficiency records. In the 1950s purchases were concentrated on Bristol 170s, Fokker Friendships and Vickers Viscount V707s and V808s. These flew for the airline for many years, with the success of the V808 demonstrated in the fact that although purchased in 1957, they were only sold as scrap by the airline in 1972. Despite the success of these planes, the dangers inherent in air travel were illustrated only too clearly in January 1952, when the airline suffered its first fatalities.

A common feature of Aer Lingus' advertising was the promotion of its fleet, especially newly purchased planes. Such planes were a subject of great fascination for the men and young boys of Ireland. Here the linking of the new Friendship, with the pages of *Eagle*, one of the best selling boy's comics of the period, shows how the advent of a new plane, at the forefront of modern aviation, was a selling point for the airline and the boy's weekly.

The blessing of the Aer Lingus fleet was an annual occurrence at Dublin airport from 1947. Additionally planes were also blessed when they joined the fleet and prior to their first flight in the Aer Lingus livery. Here, in October 1960, the Bishop of Seattle blesses a new B720 at the Boeing factory to mark Aer Lingus taking delivery of the plane.

The Vickers Viscount was a central part of the Aer Lingus fleet until the end of the 1960s, and a highly-reliable workhorse. Seen here at Dublin airport, two planes await their passengers and departure.

An Aer Lingus DC-3 flying from London to Dublin crashed in Snowdonia, Wales, killing all twenty-three people on board. It was suggested that a powerful down current of air made the plane uncontrollable, and that this caused the crash. What it did prove, was that vigilance, the constant training of staff and maintenance crews, and first-rate upkeep of the fleet, was central to a safe airline.

The next major development in the fleet came in 1958, with the opening, finally, of Aer Lingus' transatlantic route. In the first instance, the decision was made to lease aircraft for the route, simply so it could get started, and the Super-Constellation planes, that had been ordered a decade earlier, were hired. The lease agreement allowed Aer Lingus to invest in the new jet engine technology, and three Boeing 720s were ordered. The success of the transatlantic route was clear from the start. In its first year the route carried 14,781 passengers, and only four years later this number jumped to 74,360. It became clear that the B720s were not large enough, and an order was placed, again with Boeing, to purchase three B707-320Cs, which were delivered to the airline between 1965 and 1967. The traffic demand, plus increasing consumer awareness of the need to travel in comfort (especially in business and first class), led the airline to purchase its first Boeing 747, or more commonly, the jumbo jet, in 1971. These planes, while a common sight on long haul routes, and popular amongst crew and passengers, proved, apart from the peak summer season, too large for Aer Lingus' needs. They were replaced, from 1994, with the more efficient Airbus A330s that, although smaller in terms of seats, had a larger cargo hold.

The three Carvairs (converted DC4s) purchased by Aer Lingus in the early 1960s were truly something to behold. The late 1950s had witnessed a sharp rise in the number of people from Britain wishing to take holidays in Ireland with their car. To avail of the business opportunities that this afforded, the Carvairs were used to fly cars and their passengers from Dublin to Liverpool, Bristol and Cherbourg, as well as from Cork to Bristol. Unfortunately, the sight of this ungainly giant was short-lived. By 1966 the roll on-roll off ferry had been introduced, and the need to fly cars across the Irish Sea ended. The Aer Lingus Carvair left the skies. Another aviation oddity of the 1960s was

As well as promoting its services, and Ireland as a destination, Aer Lingus produced a series of posters during the 1960s and 1970s, which showed off their newly purchased planes. Such posters not only spoke to the modernity of the airline, but appealed to those of an engineering bent who were fascinated by what was new. This poster, one of the most popular plane posters the airline ever produced, detailed what they called the Boeing Shamrock Jet, and the cut through sections allowed the viewer to understand how the plane was put together and how each section worked.

The Irish launch the most exclusive club in the sky

Golden Shamrock
First Class Jet Service

With the purchase of Aer Lingus' own Boeing jet engine planes, in the early 1960s, a premium was put on providing the best first class service possible. The Golden Shamrock class, as regularly advertised in holiday magazines throughout the period, offered the most opulent means of travel between Ireland and the United States.

the prospect of supersonic travel. Although the market was eventually cornered by Concorde, the United States government had been experimenting with supersonic jets in the early 1960s, and Aer Lingus had placed a $200,000 deposit to purchase two such craft in 1964. Unfortunately the plan was abandoned by the manufacturers, and although the airline received a full return of its deposit, the spectacle of a supersonic shamrock crossing the Atlantic was lost.

With the growth of the sun holiday market in the late 1960s, Aer Lingus purchased nine Viscounts from KLM that saw service into the 1970s. The ongoing success of key routes, such as London to Dublin, saw the airline invest, from 1969, in the Boeing 737. By 1979, the number owned by Aer Lingus had risen to fourteen. These planes were so successful they were made standard on most short haul routes, and the older stock of DC3s, Viscounts and Friendships were sold off. The decision to remove the Viscounts from the Aer Lingus fleet was, in part, informed by two accidents in the late 1960s. In 1967, the Viscount, St Cathal, crashed on a training flight, with the loss of three crewmen. A year later, St Phelim, another Viscount, crashed in the Irish Sea, near Tuskar Rock, on a flight from Cork to London. All sixty-one people on board died, and despite an initial report, a further investigation was ordered into the crash in 2000. This reported in 2002, and pointed to a structural fault in the plane's tailfin as the most likely cause of the accident. The fresh report had been ordered due to long-standing rumours that the 1967 crash had in fact been caused by a collision with a British missile or drone. It remains Aer Lingus' worst ever accident.

In the 1980s, with the increase in the opening of British regional airports, and the establishment of the Aer Lingus Commuter brand, the airline purchased four Shorts 360 aircraft, which could carry thirty-five passengers, to compete effectively on these short routes. These planes saw service until the early 1990s, when they were made obsolete by economic decisions to concentrate on routes to major cities, and with the ordering, in 1987, of four Boeing 737-500 aircraft. For the routes that had smaller passenger numbers, the airline invested in four Saab 340Bs in 1991. The success of the Airbus planes on the transatlantic route, after they had replaced the jumbo jet, led to an order

Such was the interest in flying, the new buildings at Dublin airport, and the ever changing fleet of Aer Lingus, that postcards were produced by, and for, the airline and airport, to sell to their customers. This shot of a transatlantic plane being refuelled was an iconic best seller of the 1960s.

Top: Although a short-lived member of the Aer Lingus fleet, the Carvair was undoubtedly one of the most unusual planes the airline ever flew. Designed for cargo, Aer Lingus successfully employed the planes as car carriers, on Ireland to Britain routes in the years before the advent of roll on-roll off ferries. They were also used for the delivery of race horses for racing and bloodstock sales, as in this inaugural flight of horses from Cork to Cambridge.

Bottom: The annual blessing of the fleet took place at Dublin airport. In the 1950s and 1960s the blessing of the Aer Lingus fleet was a source of great fascination for the press, and regularly reported on. Although much diminished in scale, and done without the coverage of yesteryear, the airline still has its fleet blessed every year.

being placed in the late 1990s to buy the Airbus A321 to cover the Dublin to London route, which in turn have been updated with purchases of the Airbus A320. The link between Airbus and Aer Lingus has proved so important, and the planes so reliable, that the decision was made that the airline would operate its entire fleet with planes from that single manufacturer. As a result, by the summer of 2010, the Aer Lingus fleet consisted of thirty Airbus A320s and six Airbus A321s for Irish and European routes, and eight Airbus A330s for the transatlantic routes. Of these planes, 52 per cent are owned by the airline and the remainder leased.

At present, the average age of a plane in service with Aer Lingus is just over six years. With new planes already ordered, the Aer Lingus fleet will continue to be renewed and updated to best serve the routes that it flies and the needs of the passengers on board.

4 Personnel

In the early years of aviation, pilots were a source

of fascination. These men and women flying oceans and continents were the embodiment of a derring-do spirit. They were seen as fearless and, it has to be said, a little crazy, as they seemed to take their life into their hands every time they took to the air. By the time that commercial flights had begun, the image of the pilot had become a little more staid. After all, the last thing that a paying customer wanted was anyone who took risks. What was required was someone who was highly skilled, experienced, and above all, safe. That said, pilots were still seen as glamorous characters, as they did something most mere mortals could not. They could fly a plane. The appeal of the early pilot, their celebrity if you like, was evident in 1938, when the newspapers carried a story about Aer Lingus' first pilot, Oliver Armstrong. *The Irish Times* reported on 7 November 1938, that a presentation was to be made to Armstrong by the directors of the airline, to celebrate his forthcoming wedding to Vera Long, of Upper Baggot Street, Dublin. The article detailed Armstrong's career as a pilot, recounting his service with the Royal Air Force in Egypt, India and Mesopotamia, and that he had been the first to fly the Cairo to Baghdad route. By 1938, the newspaper reckoned, Armstrong had spent over 7,000 hours in the air, and had flown close to 1 million miles. It is hard to believe that the news that a pilot was to marry would make the headlines today. But such was the appeal of men like Armstrong. The early pilots were the celebrities of the day. By the late 1930s, they were no longer innovators, but they were part of a highly select and therefore fascinating group.

A big difference between the early years of Aer Lingus and now, is that all planes were flown manually with only basic technological assistance. The importance of the pilot was that their skill dictated, perhaps more than anything in those early days, whether or not the plane made it safely from airport to airport. The value of the pilot was evident in 1946, when an Aer Lingus plane flying from Shannon to Dublin suffered a malfunction that led to its starboard engine bursting into flames. On board were fifteen passengers and a crew of four. The pilot, Captain Cusack, turned back to Shannon and successfully made a safe landing, with only minor injuries occurring. The newspaper report on the incident detailed how 'young Captain Cusack, the pilot, handled his machine superbly. The Air Hostess, who is a slip of a girl, behaved with the coolness of a veteran, and all concerned conducted themselves admirably.' Cusack was like many of the other early Aer Lingus pilots who gained their flying experience either in the Royal Air Force or the Irish Air Corps. Such experience was vital, and also added to the mystique of the pilots. A challenge for all of them was moving from military to commercial craft, and also undergoing regular training as the airline constantly grew its fleet and they were asked to fly unfamiliar planes. Felim Cronin, who joined Aer Lingus as a pilot in 1961, and was made Captain in 1969, noted these ongoing changes in the fleet: 'I flew eight different aircraft over the years – from Viscounts to Carvairs and Boeings – while modern pilots would probably fly a maximum of three different aircraft throughout their career. It was a different job altogether in my day – we did a lot more manual flying – whereas today pilots need to be technical engineers as much as anything, just to monitor these high-tech computerised systems.'

For the first two decades of its existence, the growing number of pilots entering the airline usually had extensive experience, and what training was done was restricted to understanding new planes as they were taken into the fleet. Indeed, while many pilots were Irish, and had usually gained the bulk of their experience flying in other countries, a large percentage of Aer Lingus' pilots through to the 1960s were from Britain or North America. The airline put a high premium on training. In the post-war decades, as planes were added to the fleet, so pilots were sent to the aircraft manufacturer, to be trained in how to fly the new arrivals. The opening of the transatlantic route and the

For Aer Lingus, once it had opened its first route, getting the necessary personnel to expand was important. Through the late 1930s, and again after the ending of the Second World War, the airline recruited pilots from the Air Corps, the RAF and beyond. Here, in the late 1930s, a trainee is shown in his cockpit readying to fly out of Baldonnel.

Large airlines like Aer Lingus, at a major airport such as Dublin or Shannon, require a large ground staff to ensure that all the planes, on any given day, get away on time. Refuelling is a key issue, especially that many short hauls flights are only on the ground for twenty minutes or so. Back in the 1930s, the early operations at Baldonnel were a little more rudimentary. With only one or two flights a day to look after, this hand-powered refuelling truck was all that was required.

During the immediate aftermath of 11 September 2001, US airspace was closed to all inbound flights. This included one of the Aer Lingus transatlantic flights, EI-DUB. As a result, this flight amongst many other European aircraft was forced to divert to Gander. The aircraft subsequently developed a technical problem on the ground. One of my most significant memories is leading a team of engineers from Shannon, and together with colleagues from Flight Operations and Passenger Services in Dublin, we flew on another A330 to Gander. On arrival in Gander the Passenger Service team immediately went to the aid of our passengers, securing accommodation, and supplying fresh clothes and toiletries. The Flight Operation team set about getting the Aer Lingus aircraft, and therefore our passengers, out of Gander at the first available opportunity. The technical team slept on the aircraft and repaired the fault. As a result of these actions our passengers were ferried out of Gander at the earliest chance, long before many of the other European airlines.

Philip Bartlett, Line Maintenance

purchase of planes from Boeing was a case in point. Flying such long distances with a new generation of plane demanded intensive training. Throughout the late 1950s and 1960s, Aer Lingus sent its pilots on intensive courses in the United States, or else imported an American instructor to work with pilots in Ireland. The net effect was that the airline had an excellent safety record, and the skills and professionalism of its pilots were highly regarded in the world of aviation.

Such was the airline's reputation that it was able, from the late 1960s, to train pilots from other countries. This was the beginning of an expansion of the airline that would see it go beyond the business of simply flying its own planes. An important shift in the world of aviation assisted Aer Lingus in selling its expertise. The late 1960s and 1970s saw a plethora of new nations establish their own airlines. These countries, mainly in the developing nations of Africa, Asia, and Central and South America, were either in a process of rapid modernisation, or else had recently gained their independence from their former European colonisers. As such, many of them had an affinity with Aer Lingus and Ireland. It was not a mass-scale airline, like many of those in North America and elsewhere in Europe, but rather a flagship for a small nation that had grown its business from nothing. The expertise that Aer Lingus could offer, from pilots through to engineering services, was not only of the first order, but the experiences that the airline and the nation had undergone in the twentieth century were akin to those of their new customers. In 1970, Aer Lingus installed a Boeing 737 simulator at Dublin airport that, when not being used by its own staff, was offered to pilots from other airlines. These came from old aviation nations such as the United States, Britain and Holland, as well as from those new countries just starting out, namely Algeria, Uganda, Jordan, Bahamas, Lebanon, Malta, Kenya, Tanzania and Zambia.

The outsourcing of Aer Lingus' skill base was not restricted to its pilots. From the early days of Baldonell, Aer Lingus had done as much servicing of its own planes as was practically possible. It built a solid reputation in the field, and an apprenticeship in the airline's engineering department was seen as a highly desirable and skilled job for someone freshly out of school or college. The success and reputation of the airline's engineering department was such, that from 1969 it began selling its services to other companies. What began with a contract with Trans Polar of Norway and Trans European of Belgium grew quickly so that by the end of the 1970s, Aer Lingus was responsible for the aircraft maintenance of the planes of Bahama Air, Cameroon Airways, Royal Air Moroc, Air Guinea and Nigeria Airways, as well as fleets from Bangladesh and Zambia.

The reach of the Aer Lingus knowledge was such, that many start-up airlines in far-flung corners of the world would contract the Irish operator to provide the entire management staff to oversee the running of their business as they began. As a result, Aer Lingus managers found themselves transplanted from the familiar surroundings of Dublin or Shannon, and instead were running airlines such as Air Zambia, Kenya Airways, LIAT in Antigua, Ghana Airways and ALM in the Dutch Antilles, and had a significant presence at Air Jamaica and Guyana Airways. By the mid-1970s, over forty airlines worldwide were

94

As Aer Lingus grew in the late 1940s, so it moved its flying operations from Baldonnel to Dublin airport, and many of its ground staff began working from the airline's new offices on O'Connell Street, Dublin. This picture, taken in the late 1940s, shows the front of house booking staff on the European desk.

relying on Aer Lingus expertise, and this ranged from management skills, through pilots and pilot training, cabin crew training, catering, ground handling, aircraft maintenance and aircraft leasing.

The aviation industry has always been driven by technology, and the advent of computer systems in the 1960s were a boon to airlines. In the use of computers, Aer Lingus was at the forefront of developments. In 1969, it invested in a real-time system, ASTRAL, which controlled the reservations system and made the booking of seats, as well as an awareness of how routes were functioning, much faster and more informed than the old system. Aer Lingus was only the second airline in the world to invest in such a system, and the move was recognised by the government as a major step forward. The airline was contracted by the government to introduce data processing into its various departments, and it formed a new company, Airline Systems Services, to sell its computer and reservations expertise across the industry. For Aer Lingus, the importance of ASTRAL was that they knew minute by minute how many seats were filled on their different planes. This enabled them to sell their spare capacity to other airlines, and by selling the computerised reservations service to airlines across the world, it enabled the Aer Lingus name to have a global presence.

Aer Lingus has been a major employer within, and beyond the Irish state. This picture, from 1961, shows a group of newly recruited staff receiving their training. All of the women depicted here would have been single, and once they made the decision to marry (prior to the late 1970s), they would have had to leave their job.

Anne Cronley was a well known TV and radio beauty consultant, and was hired by the airline in the in 1966, to teach sales staff in Cork, Dublin and Limerick how to groom so that they looked their best. All women attending the courses were introduced to staff dress regulations, appropriate hairstyles, deportment, and make-up. As *Aer Scéala* concluded, 'good grooming reflects the go-ahead company image of efficiency'.

Of the many investments made by Aer Lingus in other businesses, including tour operations and hotels, the most successful and, given the future of the airline industry, most enlightened, was the 45 per cent stake it purchased in Guinness Peat Aviation (GPA). Based at Shannon, GPA became a major player in the world of aircraft broking and leasing. Not only did the move create profits for the company, but it also ensured a favoured position for the airline as the training and maintenance that was required by GPA customers was done by Aer Lingus. Further acquisitions followed, including the purchase of Irish Helicopters in 1974 and the long lease of fourteen flagship hotels in the United States. By the mid-1970s, the various services provided by Aer Lingus to other airlines, and the success of the businesses that they had bought into, had made what the airline termed its ancillary activities hugely profitable. While the core business of flying paying passengers was always subject to the swings of the economy and the demands of customers, the ancillary activities provided Aer Lingus, during the 1970s and into the 1980s, with a core profit each year. This was important as it shielded the airline from the worst effects of the downturn in the global economy, the high cost of oil and the impact on air travel of political instability around the world. The selling of the skills of the airline's staff, and the wider investments that the company made, ensured, not just the survival, but the prosperity of Aer Lingus. By 1978, Aer Lingus employed over 6,000 people and was the state's largest exporting company earning £120 million overseas. In its support for, and investment in Ireland as a tourist destination, it also supported the livelihoods of some 30,000 people connected with the tourism business at home.

The growth in the Aer Lingus engineering business was evidenced in the early 1980s when it opened Airmotive. This was an engine overhaul business, and while servicing the Aer Lingus fleet, this was only a fraction of the business. Throughout the 1980s, Airmotive successfully filled its order books with work from other airlines, so that 75 per cent of its business was in servicing foreign planes. Other moves to diversify the business in the 1980s included the establishment of Devtec, which was a research and development business, ALD Commercial Services, which provided financial leases for the airline and hotel industry in the United States, PARC Hospital Management, which provided and managed nursing and technical staff for medical clinics, ATS Robotics in Canada, Cara Data Processing and the Copthorne Hotel group, which was sold in 1996 for over £200 million. The success of the diversification, which had taken the airline from flying passengers to training the pilots of other airlines and even providing medical services, was evidenced when the strategy was a decade old. In the ten years since their foundation, ancillary activities had made the airline a net profit of £110 million.

In the late 1980s, Aer Lingus decided to reorganise its aircraft servicing and engineering business. TEAM (Targeting for Excellence in Aircraft Maintenance) Aer Lingus was a bold venture, but also one that demonstrated how fragile, despite its successes, the process of diversification could be. In the rapidly changing economy of the 1990s, it became apparent that a business that had become as large and diverse as Aer Lingus would be difficult to sustain. In 1990, the airline withdrew from the tour-operating business, and this was the first stage of a process of retreat that would last into the 2000s. In August 1990, the Iraqi invasion of Kuwait, and the ensuing Gulf War, destabilised the aviation industry. By the end of 1992, Aer Lingus, given a disastrous few months in terms of passengers, and falling profits across its ancillary businesses, was losing money and recorded a loss in excess of £10 million. There was an obvious need for the company to refocus on what its core business was – flying – and the company was reorganised into four divisions: Passenger, Cargo, Airline Services and Hotels and Commercial Holdings. While this refocusing would, in time, stabilise Aer Lingus, the message was clear: the airline had to withdraw from its non-core businesses. TEAM Aer Lingus was a case in point. In its first year, the strategy of bringing the airline's servicing businesses together under one umbrella seemed a good move. The company recorded a profit, and had managed to attract significant new customers, such as Virgin Atlantic. However, against the backdrop of wider political and economic instability, and the swift rate of change in the airline industry, the airline servicing business changed. More decisions were being made on the basis of cost, particularly important to the new breed of low cost airlines, and Aer Lingus' reputation for excellence in aircraft servicing mattered for little. By 1994, TEAM Aer Lingus was losing money, and by 1998, the decision was

Every day before flying, Aer Lingus pilots have to check in with the operations department, to confirm their routes for the day, the weather and any other impediments or delays they might face. This picture, from the early 1960s, shows a pilot taking his instructions from operations for the day. The period was one of renewed expansion at Dublin airport, and through the window the scaffolding for another new building can be seen.

AerSceala

YESTERDAY FACES

From our photo archives

■ *In this selection from the photo files many faces will be recognised only by older staff. Some of them are still with us. Some have retired or, sadly, have since died. A few of the very young faces may have since joined the ranks of our serving staff. They could be labelled "Tomorrow*

Aer Lingus has a long tradition in aeronautical engineering. Prior to outsourcing, the airline carried out all of its own plane maintenance, and a job in Aer Lingus' engineering department was seen as highly desirable, indeed, was an occupation chosen by generations of the same family. Gathered here are the engineers of the 1950s attending a staff meeting: the men who were the key to keeping the airline in the sky.

For something as modern as an airline, communication is essential. During the refitting of Baldonnel, ready for the inaugural flight in 1936, it became clear to the airline that they could not get a phone line as the airport was too far from the exchange. Access to phone lines was problematic for many businesss in Ireland, through to the 1970s, but Aer Lingus was luckier than most. Through its offices on O'Connell Street and at Dublin airport, it was able to install the lines it needed and a major switchboard operation, with trained telephonists.

310002/1 UNIT REPLACEMENT CONTROL RECORD   T.D. 1033

	INSTALLED			REMOVED				
DATE	A/c. REG	TOTAL PLANE HRS.	PLANE HRS. CHANGE AT	DATE	REASON	TOTAL PLANE HRS.	HRS. OF SERVICE	TOTAL Service Hrs.

Received Installed Douglas Aircraft OY-DDO (FB) 12·11·48   2866 2866

Hrs. FB/S. 2866= 8000= 20·6·49 During Conversion   3001· 3001=
Removed and thoroughly Inspected, Doublers and Angles
Inspected to Douglas Drll. 243, Complete new set of attach angles bolts.
Mainplane reassembled and Reinstalled Refer o/Haul Report MP1/3/6/49/0   6977 6977

20·6·49 FB/S. 3001= 8000· 29·4·52 Scheduled @ Ck 9
o/Haul of mainplane completed Refer o/Haul Reft No MP1/3/52/0   1800 8777

30·4·52 FB/S 6977 10977/14977 11·4·53 To facilitate O/S Rework @ Ck 8
Wing attach angles Doublers & bolts inspected. Next inspn. due @ 12777 A/c Hours

15·5·53 FB/S 8777 12777/14977 Doublers inspn. reduced to 3600 Hrs
15·5·53 FB/S 8777 12371/14977 30/10/55 For Doubler Insp. Card 45/11 (MP/4/11/55/R) 3528 12305
Doubler Inspection Carried out as per Douglas Directive

31/10/55 AFB/S 12325 14977 Increased by 15%. Ref EI 40/56 50/12/4 O+Reworked 9/7/ 16005 16005
31/10/55 AFB/S 14174 N.D/17224 4/12/56 Schd for Rework
9/12/57 MR/S 16134 20134/25334 1·2·60 Dble. Insp Carried Out as per Dir 39/24/1 3178 19183

UNIT	SERIAL No.	MAKER			7,000 8000	O.H. DUE 15/4/56 9200

| | 1 | 2 | 3 | 4 | 5 | 6 | 7 | 8 | 9 | 10 |

Wing; Attach Angles; Bolts W/S/7007 DOUGLAS.

Like the family car, but only more often and with greater precision, all planes in the Aer Lingus fleet have been regularly serviced. In an age before computerisation, this service sheet from the 1950s shows how diligently its Douglas planes were serviced (*courtesy of Angela Murphy*).

made to sell the business to the Danish company, FLS. A decade later, the Swiss firm, SR Technics, which had bought FLS, closed its facility at Dublin airport, and the long tradition of aviation servicing and engineering, which had begun with Aer Lingus in 1936, and had been carried on by the airline for nearly sixty years, shrank back dramatically in size. The mid-1990s also saw the airline sell its interests in Irish Helicopters, its technology companies and the bulk of its hotels. The decision, in 1992, to float the airline leasing business, GPA, on the stock market, against the backdrop of the Gulf War, was a disaster, and caused losses to Aer Lingus of £40 million.

Despite the negative impact of removing itself from its ancillary businesses, the positive was that Aer Lingus refocused on its core business: being an airline. Although conditions in the 1990s and into the 2000s were difficult, the refocus paid dividends. In 1996 alone, Aer Lingus was voted Airline of the Year, as well as best airline in the UK for transatlantic flights and for business customers.

While the variety of interests and spheres of operation that Aer Lingus works in is reduced from the 1970s and 1980s, one thing is clear: the airline functioned as an innovator, and worked as a key force in world aviation in terms of providing training for personnel and services for the industry. Across the world to this day, there are planes flying that were maintained and serviced by Aer Lingus, pilots and crew who were trained in Dublin, and management structures and skills that were learnt from the Irish. The size and scale of Aer Lingus' activities over the years has been breathtaking. Those activities made Ireland a key centre for the world's aviation industry, and meant that while the airline itself may have had a specific series of routes in the northern hemisphere, its reach, in terms of the knowledge that it sold on, was global. All that activity did not stop innovation at home. Aer Lingus has continued to train its own staff, and in the pilot area it proved a forward-thinker in terms of gender. The cockpit, perhaps because of the legacy of the Second World War and the number of ex-Air Force pilots who went to work for commercial airlines, was seen as a male bastion. In 1973, Emily Warner had become the first woman commercial pilot, flying with Frontier Airlines in the United States, and she had been followed by the first women pilots in Europe with SAS. On 27 September 1977, Grainne Cronin became the first woman pilot with Aer Lingus, a full decade before British Airways took the same step. Cronin was aware she was entering a male world, and recalled: 'It wasn't easy, I have to say, entering such a male-dominated arena, but Aer Lingus were very forward-thinking for the time.' She was joined in the following two years by two more women pilots. To mark her retirement in 2010, Cronin flew an Airbus A330 from Dublin to Boston, accompanied by Captain Elaine Egan and First Officer Shelley Gahan in the cockpit, making it an all-woman crew. Cronin had piloted the airline's first all-woman crew in 1988. In 2007, Aer Lingus made Davina Pratt its first woman Chief Pilot, and she was placed in charge of the airline's 530 pilots, 40 of whom were women. Pratt, a past pupil of Wilson's Hospital School, Multyfarnham, started working for Aer Lingus after finishing college, and was aware of the world she was entering: 'I joined aviation knowing it was a career dominated by men. It's a bit like a man going into nursing; you know that's the way it is. From day one, I recognised that fact. I've just mucked in and got on with it. I don't see people in terms of men or women. And, in Aer Lingus, I've never been treated as anything other than a pilot.'

By the end of the summer 2010, Aer Lingus employed over 3,500 people, including 465 pilots, 1,205 cabin crew and 234 in maintenance. Despite the upheavals in the airline industry and the wider economy, Aer Lingus remains a desirable place to work, and one that continues, through the efforts of all its personnel, to offer one of the best safety records in aviation and the friendly Irish service that has been a benchmark of its history on its own flights and in the training it has offered to airlines across the world.

Selling Aer Lingus during the 1950s and 1960s depended on a variety of visual prompts. Many of these had to do with the destinations to which the airline flew, and others hung on the modernity of the fleet. Here, as in many other posters, it is the personnel that are pushed centre stage to emphasise the welcoming nature of the airline.

Each time Aer Lingus prepared to take ownership of a new plane, its staff had to be trained accordingly. From the early 1960s, on the transatlantic route, all the new planes came from Boeing and, as a result, Burbank, California, the home of Boeing, became a regular place for airline staff for training. This shot from the early 1960s shows stewardesses examining the engines of a newly purchased Boeing.

Until the 1980s and 1990s, getting to Dublin airport and boarding a flight was a novel experience for many people. Often people were not sure of what to do or where to go once they had checked in. Here, ground crew wearing the Digby Morton designed outfit, in the early 1970s, helped passengers through the complexities of the newly expanded Dublin airport.

OVERSEAS WORKSHOP DEVELOPMENT

One of the main areas where Aer Lingus has assisted developing airlines in the past has been in workshop development. A recent addition to the range of Aer Lingus Technical Services is our TASC program of workshop development which adopts the modular approach to the buildup of facilities at the customers base. Detailed information on the TASC system is available on request.

TECHNICAL TRAINING

Our Technical Training School provides a wide range of training services including "Type" Licence courses; Apprentice Training; Specialist On the Job training and Production Planning and Control Courses.

We offer over sixty "Type" courses and specialise in Apprentice Training to Irish Licence Authority or C.A.A. standard. These courses combine professional theoretical instruction with excellent "hands on" experience in our approved hangars and workshops.

In the late 1960s, Aer Lingus began selling its expertise to airlines around the world. One of its key strengths was engineering, and in this 1970s brochure for the airline's services, its ability to train staff from other countries was foregrounded.

5 Cabin Crew

In December 1945, Aer Lingus made an announcement that brought the prospect of a glamorous, jet-setting life closer to the women of Ireland. The potentially life-changing announcement was that Aer Lingus was looking for what were then termed Air Hostesses. The newspapers were fascinated, and took delight in listing the attributes necessary. As *The Irish Times* reported on 20 December 1945, 'here are some of the qualifications necessary for girls who have the ambition to become air hostesses – Age, between 21 and 26; height, 5 ft 2 ins to 5 ft 6 ins; weight, 7½ stone to 9 stone. And of course the girls must be attractive, intelligent, and have personality and charm. While not absolutely essential, a knowledge of languages, especially Irish and French, will be regarded as an important asset to applicants.' The newspaper, while fascinated by the search for the airline's Air Hostesses, a story it would return to regularly during 1946, clearly believed the glamour of the job outweighed any sense that it was real work. It offered the opinion that, 'the duties are not onerous. They consist mainly of looking after passengers and serving meals on the plane.'

Given the appeal of the job, especially in a depressed post-war Irish economy that traditionally had few interesting employment opportunities for young women, Aer Lingus was inundated with applicants. Over 900 applications were received. In the event, by June 1946, four women, what one newspaper referred to as 'the lucky ones', were the first group to be selected by the airline, and they had begun their training. The four were revealed as a nurse, a radiologist and two secretaries. Their training lasted for six to eight weeks. Week one allowed them to familiarise themselves with the plane on which they would work, and once they had the necessary insurance, they were taken on local flights to, as one correspondent reported, 'overcome nervousness and sickness'. Once they had been in the air, the women were given instructions in parachuting (clearly by now over the nervousness), lifebelt drill and fire-fighting. They were toured through the airport to meet the airline's departments on the ground, and also put through a first aid course that ended with a written examination. Once they had completed every stage of this training, they were ready to take to the air.

Despite the hype surrounding this 'first' intake of Air Hostesses, these were not actually the original women to fill the role. On a Christmas flight from Dublin to Liverpool in 1939, Eva Toner from the publicity department of the airline had acted as unofficial hostess and, from 26 December 1945, just as the press were salivating over the first open advertisement for the positions, Aer Lingus put its initial three hostesses – Shelia Broderick, Angela Cogan and Maureen Fogerty – to work on the Dublin to London route. For those first women who staffed the cabins of the planes, pay ranged from £3 and ten shillings to £5 per week, depending on experience. Considering how small the capacity was on post-war flights, the stewardess to passenger ratio was very high, and the service was considered exemplary. The airline quickly developed a good reputation for its on-flight service and for the quality of its staff.

The place that the steward occupies is a fascinating one. Apart from check-in staff, who we deal with less and less in this age of online check-in, the on-board staff are the only human interaction most of us have with an airline. Passengers may hear announcements from the pilot of the plane, but we do not meet them, and neither are the baggage handlers, dispatchers, operations, controllers or administrative staff introduced. The steward is therefore in a perhaps unenviable position. To the passengers they are *the* face of an airline. This was well understood by Aer Lingus when they began hiring stewardesses. These women, for they were all women then (men were only introduced as stewards from 1978), were the embodiment of the airline. As such they had to be what one early internal document referred to as 'the best of Irish woman-hood'. Given the Catholicism of the Irish state, the limits set on the roles for women by the Constitution of 1937, and the boundaries set by social practice and social conservatism, the first generations of stewardesses were expected

Following the first open advertisement for positions in 1946, stewardesses were a source of fascination for the newspapers. The *Irish Press* featured this shot in 1947, showing five of the early recruits to the airline on their inaugural flight.

Until boarding gates came into being in the 1950s, early Aer Lingus passengers were checked off a clipboard list of their names, as they crossed from terminal to plane. In 1948, Rita Hewitt was charged with the job of checking that the people on the tarmac were indeed the passengers who were supposed to be travelling.

I remember coming home after being caught-up in the first Gulf War for three months while working for Aer Lingus in Kuwait. From the time we landed in London Heathrow from Jordan we were inundated with goodwill from Aer Lingus staff in Heathrow, then by the crew on the flight home to Dublin, in Dublin airport at the great reception Aer Lingus hosted in the VIP lounge in Dublin airport. Subsequently, we learned of the tireless efforts by our colleagues in Aer Lingus to ensure our safety while in Kuwait/Iraq and their efforts to contact us and to keep our families informed of our circumstances. I felt humble and very proud to work with such great people.

Cormac Costello, Information Technology

to be attractive, but they had also to be the height of respectability. Representing the airline, the nation and a national morality were the key to a successful stewardess. To enforce a sense of demure correctness, a strict set of rules was put in place, and Pat Blake, a woman who had served in the British army during the war, was put in charge, as Manager of the Hostess Branch. The rule book was extensive and, for the early stewardesses, included: a ban on dating customers, a strict dress code, a prohibition on consuming alcohol, chewing gum and smoking, instructions that hostesses were not to cycle to work, and twice-yearly tests in Irish and French (increments were withheld if the results were unsatisfactory). The first uniform, which appeared in late 1945, consisted of skirt, white shirt, jacket and cap and was coloured brown, rather than the green we now associate with the airline. As with other jobs within the broad state sector, once married, a hostess had to resign her position and take her place in the family. Some did disobey the rules, and met their future husbands on board. Ciaran O'Reilly recalled how his parents met:

Mum [Maire Cavanagh] joined Aer Lingus in 1955 and left in 1957 to marry my father, Terence. They had met in autumn 1955 when he and four pals turned up unannounced on her otherwise

Cabin Crew

empty DC3 positioning back to Dublin out of Tabres, France. She, assuming them in the circumstances to be company employees hitching a ride home, initially took a shockingly casual approach to their in-flight service: they were told there were refreshments down the back and invited to help themselves. Happily, such familiarity bred romance. Dad, soon outed as a Tyrone accountant, later sat with her at the rear and helped her do petty cash. Back on terra firma telephone numbers were exchanged (in those days a hanging offence) out of sight of the ever-watchful supervisors and the rest, as they say, is history.

For the first women to join Aer Lingus, the job, despite the rules that were in place, represented a real sense of freedom. They were young, single women, employed to carry out a glamorous and quite unique job. Of the first stewardesses employed, very few had ever been more than a few miles beyond their home, and only one or two had ever flown. The main instruction they were given was to keep the passengers comfortable and, as one recalled years later, to avoid conversations that dealt with 'politics, religion or anything risqué. Half of us didn't know what risqué meant.' With the passing years, so the role of the stewardesses changed. On the early flights, there was no service to be done. At first flasks of coffee were introduced, which the stewardesses had to serve, followed by sandwiches and eventually a full bar service. Due to the configuration of the planes (the aisles were very narrow), and the expectations of service in the 1940s and 1950s, there was no such thing as trolley service. All hostesses were trained how to deliver food and drink to the customer from a tray. This individual attention and eye on detail was something for which Aer Lingus quickly gained a reputation. Maree Sheehy, one the first six hostesses to work for Aer Lingus, recalled her sense of pride when interviewed in 1981: 'we felt we were lifting Ireland out of its obscurity. Wherever we went we felt we were representing the country and we were proud of it. Later on, when I saw the first Constellation flying in, there were tears in my eyes.' The early stewardesses were aware of their unique position. Aileen Turley recalled that 'we had a tremendous amount of publicity and everyone knew who you were.

The women who were selected to train as cabin crew in the 1940s and 1950s were, by virtue of the small numbers involved, part of an elite. These women were the successful class of 1958 and were (from left to right): Anne Swaine, Hanne Jorgensen, Maureen Hodgins, Cynthia Guise-Brown, Olive Regan, Patricia Reynolds and Betty Conlon.

4,000 GIRLS SAID YES TO OUR PROPOSAL

When you have to operate on a spartan advertising budget you've got to put in some hard creative thinking to get the maximum value for the little money you have to play with. That's what the Personnel Department did recently when they launched a series of advertisements for new hostesses in the national press. The hard-thinking produced some refreshingly original ads. They leaped out of the page, grabbed the girls and brought them along in their thousands to a series of downtown, walk-in interviews in a number of Dublin hotels. Sure, they created a lot of work for the team of interviewers, but they had a wider field of choice from which to select this year's intake of some 200 new hostesses.

" Are you running an airline or a matrimonial agency "? one caller asked Head of Employment and Employee Services Cóilín O Broin. He was referring to what was probably the most daring ad. in the series. It invited girls to " make a date with us now and this summer you could be walking down the aisle ". It alludes to an aircraft aisle, of course, but the proverb says " There's many a true word spoken in jest ". Every year Cupid has a real big shoot-up among our highly marriageable hostesses.

Does Mr. O Broin usually get 'phone calls about his advertisements. " No ", he says, " but this year our advertising seems to have created a stir among staff and the general public. Many people have complimented us on the attractiveness and effectiveness of the series ".

The fact that almost 4,000 hopeful young ladies answered the call is one measure of the ads' effectiveness. They caught the eye of "Tatler's Parade" in the "Irish Independent" too. It's a welcome —and well deserved—bonus to a job well done when the columnists give your campaign the spotlight treatment!

The desirability of a job on Aer Lingus cabin crew, coupled with the recession of the 1970s, meant that the airline was inundated when it advertised its openings in 1972. *Aer Scéala* was delighted with the high number of applicants and the advertising campaign that had brought them flocking in. It is doubtful that some of the advertising copy would pass unremarked today.

Cabin crew have regularly been used by photographers to model the latest design or to promote goods. In 1950, Yvonne McTernan, a stewardess from Ennis, was chosen by the American photographer, Ben Stahl, to pose for him. He was compiling a collection of photographs, of women from around the world, that he felt best represented the women of their country. After McTernan was chosen, *Aer Scéala* offered the opinion that, 'the choicest selection of typically Irish girls are in the airline'.

Shelia Hampson was an Aer Lingus stewardess who was chosen, in 1961, to be photographed to promote the airline's transatlantic services. She was photographed at various New York locations, including the mecca of Irish weekend shoppers, Macy's (*courtesy of Shelia Hampson*).

I suppose if you compare the '40s, with the Aer Lingus of today, it would be like the difference between a family grocer and a supermarket.' Being selected as a stewardess was, for most women, like winning the employment lottery. Terry Prone has written about the desirability of the job for women of her generation, recalling how, 'at secondary school, every other career came second to the idea of being an Aer Lingus air hostess. When they announced they had vacancies, every favour was pulled by mothers and fathers to get their daughter at least as far as the interviews. When someone we knew was accepted, it was like they'd been assumed into heaven. From then on, they would be jetting around the world, living in hotels and tanning themselves on resort beaches until they fell in love with an Aer Lingus pilot.'

One of the biggest changes for the cabin crew, as for the rest of the airline's employees, was the opening of transatlantic routes in 1958. Rather than dealing with short flights to Britain and the rest of Europe, the cabin crew were working longer flights and dealing with the problems of time changes and jet lag. Despite the different conditions, Aer Lingus prided itself on the standards of service it set across the Atlantic. This stretched from the opulent surroundings of the Golden Shamrock first class service that was inaugurated with the arrival of the first Boeing jet engine planes, right through to the care and attention that was given to those flying economy. The presence of the cabin crew, and their helpful interactions with passengers, are central to many people's memories of flying Aer Lingus. As Mike Farragher wrote in the *Irish Voice*:

> We made the pilgrimage to Ireland every other year to see the grandparents in the '70s, and I remember well the goddesses who sashayed down the aisles with their green pencil skirts and tight overflowing blouses. They looked like Bond girls; tall, cute and cultured, they had velvety voices kissed by the hint of an Irish brogue. It was the kind of accent that transcended any region. There were no Dublin 'Iuvs' or Galway 'cratures' … a possible product of some Aer Lingus covert accent finishing school that sanded down the rougher spots of the Irish tongue. They gave you the royal treatment no matter what class of ticket you bought.

Top: Until the mid-1970s, there was an annual Miss London Airport contest. Each year, Aer Lingus would select an employee to represent the airline in the competition. In 1963, Miss Fitzgerald, a traffic clerk, was selected by the airline to represent them in London.
Bottom: In 1967 he was the best known Irish man playing football, and regarded as the fifth Beatle. As part of its St Patrick's Day celebrations, Aer Lingus flew fresh shamrock to Manchester to present to George Best. Mary Kilroy was the stewardess chosen to hand over the basket to the great player.

In an age before screens were placed in every headrest, and multi channel in-flight entertainment began, passengers were not aware of where in the sky they were. Whereas now we can check the in-flight mapping system to locate our plane, back in the 1960s, young aviators relied on a stewardess and a globe to know where they were.

The service mentality, which had stretched from its genesis in the late 1940s to the years of the transatlantic jumbo jet, was a product of the airline's culture. Ann Sulzman, who began working for Aer Lingus in 1958, recalled that, 'we were told to think of the aircraft as our drawing room and the passengers as our guests. We weren't allowed to call them "sir" or "madam". We had to address them by their names, which we usually found out by discreetly checking the name tags on men's briefcases and the ladies coats.' For many passengers of the airline, it was the small details, especially for those who had never flown before, that were memorable, and speak to a different age than today's efficiency. Food, as mentioned, was served off trays. Hot towels were presented to each passenger, to allow them to freshen up before landing, and hard-boiled sweets were handed out to stop ears from getting blocked as pressure changed. Prior to the mid-1960s and the longer range of the airline's fleet, planes were slower than they are now. Many flights, whether into Europe or across the Atlantic, had to stop for refueling en route, and on such stops there was no disembarkation into a warm lounge. It was the job of the cabin crew to pamper the passengers while they were stationary, and to keep passengers' minds off the delay to their travels. Although air crew would be seen by many people as having glamorous and desirable jobs, their pay in the early decades (before they became unionised in early 1950s) was, in line with other work for women, low. The advent of duty free sales on board offered one perk for the cabin crew. Those working on any given flight were awarded 5 per cent of the duty free bar sales, and 10 per cent for the person that sold the most. The reality was, for many of the cabin crew, that their job, while having definite perks, did not offer huge financial rewards. Despite this, the mystique of the stewardess lasted well into the 1980s. It was seen as a glamorous job, and as a result the media was always fascinated. Aer Lingus stewardesses were regularly used for promotional work by the airline to sell its services, as well as by fashion photographers who needed an ideal clothes horse for the latest range of Donegal tweeds and suchlike. Even film documentary makers took an interest in what it took to be a stewardess, and in 1957, one of the series of the Eyes of Ireland films, made under the flagship of Gael Linn's *Amharc Éireann* films, was dedicated to them. *Mná Spéire* (Air Hostess Training) was the twelfth film

Top: Serving in first class, on transatlantic routes, was the goal of many cabin crew employed by the airline. Here, a stewardess serves the elite on a transatlantic flight in the early 1960s.

Bottom: To celebrate Aer Lingus' twenty-first anniversary, the airline mounted an exhibition in London. To engage the public, a mock-up of a Viscount cabin was installed. The hostess in the foreground, assisting the man with his in-flight magazine is Marie Cavanagh, who met her future husband on board a flight in 1955 (*courtesy of Ciaran O'Reilly*).

AER LINGUS – IRISH

HOSTESS ROSTER

Two weeks commencing MONDAY JULY 6 1970

CONTINENTAL & PROVINCIAL — **EUROPEAN**

STAFF NO.	NAME	DAY DATE	MON 6	TUES 7	WED 8	THUR 9	FRI 10	SAT 11	SUN 12	MON 13	TUES 14	WED 15	THUR 16	FRI 17	SAT 18	SUN 19
16192	MORRIN	M						12K 314	Roc 20-06	SD	SD		Zero00	514	
15029	MOTT	S	SD												
12883	CLARKE	P	SN158-16	SN150											
17488	DONEGAN	M	SN154	(SD)											
12186	EAGLE	P	SD												
1290	HEARY	E	SN154												
11376	HEALY	M	SN162			SN158									
17733	LYONS	M			SN154										
13878	O'CONNOR	C	SN162												
1217	O'TOOLE	H	SN166												
11493	BANNAN	M													
16294	BERGIN	N													
1655	BOLAND	S													
16656	CAHILL	I													
16523	COLLERAN	N													
16659	COLLINS	M													
16090	COMERFORD	A													
16661	DEMPSEY	K													
15466	DENNY	J													
14039	DORAN	M													
16664	DOYLE	HP													
16665	EGAN	C													
16666	GUY	G													
16667	HAMMERSTEIN	M													
1669	HAMMERSTEIN	V													
16528	HANNON	F													
16529	HASSENSTEIN	C													
1670	HUGHES	P													
16300	KEARNEY	N													
16301	LAWLOR	N													
16303	MAHON	G													
16304	MASSIMI	N													
16308	MOLLOY	CM													
16992	MURPHY	A													
16478	McDONALD	MG													
1621	McGEOHN	A													
16526	McGETTIGAN	M													
16724	O'HALLORAN	S													
16122	O'RIORDAN	I													
15519	O'SHEA	E													
16533	O'SULLIVAN	A													
16996	PFEIFFER	M													
16124	QUINN	A													
16319	ROONEY	B													
16495	SHERIDAN	B													
16321	SHORTALL	M													
16127	VAUGHAN	D													
16128	WHITNEY	E													
16315	NEYLIN	J	SDS	TFN											

PREPARED BY Gabriel Lee

CPS

PAGE 1 OF 4

DO/4/A

In the 1940s, Irish newspapers, while fascinated by the idea of stewardesses, did not believe that they actually did much work. By the 1970s the situation had transformed dramatically. Rather than one or two flights a day, Aer Lingus planes criss-crossed the skies on busy schedules. This work scheduling sheet from 1970, shows how detailed the plans for staff were, and how their two days off a week were far from a weekend affair (*courtesy of Kay O'Rourke*).

in the series, and was hugely popular at the time. Watching it now, it seems quaintly dated and rather conservative. The attention in training seems to be more on service than issues of safety or efficiency. And while there are still rules for how a member of cabin crew should appear today, 1950s lessons on personal grooming and make-up speak volumes about the social conservatism of the time, and yet the concomitant level of glamour that was expected.

For many people who flew and worked on the transatlantic flights, the arrival of the jumbo jet was a highpoint in terms of the sense of indulgence that flying could offer. As the *Irish Independent* recalled, 'the sky over Shannon turned pink with pride at all this cosmopolitan elegance. Caviar and lobster thermidor were served on Tara china, accompanied by Irish linen napery, Newbridge silver cutlery and crystal glasswear. The planes were seldom full, the passengers were mostly men and they were usually very rich. They needed to be, considering that a return fare to New York in 1975 would have set them back £900 when a generous week's wages was £35.' On the jumbo jet, the cabin crew were regarded as angels in the sky, and Aer Lingus won many awards for its on-board service.

By the 1960s, Aer Lingus was a well-known and well-respected airline brand. At a time when new air travel markets were being opened in regions such as the Caribbean, Africa and Asia, many of the emerging national airlines from those countries came to Aer Lingus to be trained. Such provision of training, as part of the Aer Lingus history, is often remembered in terms of technical and engineering skills, but even here cabin crew were active. In June 1968, a team from Aer Lingus comprising Ann Boyle (Assistant Chief Hostess – Atlantic), Marian McCreery (Hostess Training Officer) and Patricia Reynolds (Senior Hostess) were responsible for training the newly hired cabin crews who would work the planes of Air Bahama, which was due to take to the air a month later. Air Bahama's in-house journal recalled that, 'Irish passengers flying on the world's newest airline – International Air Bahama – should not be too surprised if they get a "cead mile failte", a thousand million greetings, from any of the new hostesses. For the girls have just completed an Aer Lingus course similar to that given to Irish hostesses.' The Air Bahama crew were not the first stewardesses that Aer Lingus had trained, but they were certainly the

CARE AND CLEANING OF UNIFORM ITEMS (WOMEN)

Proper care and cleaning of uniform items is important to ensure each item continues to look its best.

Winter Tweed Jacket/Skirt   :   Dry clean only.

Summer Jacket/Skirt   :   Dry clean only.

Coat/Cape   :   Dry clean only.

Hat: If the hat becomes wet, shake off excess moisture and dry away from direct heat. If cleaning is necessary, dry-clean only.

Scarf: It is recommended that the scarf be dry-cleaned at its first laundering to settle the dyes. On subsequent launderings, it can be hand-washed safely.

Winter Uniform Blouse: Machine washable. The manufacturers recommend that the blouse be ironed when medium damp to ensure a crisp appearance.

Summer Uniform Blouse: The following care instructions from Courtalds fabrics. " 40 degrees C wash on synthetic cycle or handwash in warm water. Ironing should be carried out on the single dot setting, best results are achieved if ironed damp. Although the fabric is produced to the highest international standard of colourfastness and fully tested in our laboritries it is strongly advisable to wash dark colours of this type seaperately from light. In common with cotton viscose is a cellulosic fibre and therefore displays similar flammability properties".

Slipover: Made from 100% lambswool, this item needs special care. It can be handwashed at 40 degrees. Dry flat away from direct heat. Dry iron at a warm to cool setting. It can also be dry-cleaned. Do not bleach, machine wash, wring, tumble/spin dry, or steam iron.

Cardigan Jacket: This is also a woollen item which needs delicate handling.
It can be hand-washed at 40 degrees. Dry flat and away from direct heat. Dry iron at a cool setting. It can also be dry cleaned. **Do not** bleach, machine wash, wring tumble/spin dry, or steam iron.

Both of the above items carry cleaning instructions on the manufacturers label attached to the garment's neckband. These instructions, in the form of symbols, are described and elaborated above. They must be adhered to.

From the early days of the airline, when Pat Blake ruled the appearance and conduct of the original stewardesses with a firm hand, there have always been dress codes for those working at Aer Lingus. Rules included not only what to wear and in what setting, but also how each item of clothing should be cared for and cleaned. This booklet of regulations was issued to all staff in the 1990s.

Aer Lingus not only trained its own cabin crew, but also many others from airlines all over the world. The training was done at Dublin airport, and included time becoming familiar with the on-board service. This included the cabin crew acting as guinea pigs for each other, to learn how dinner was served.

largest number from a start-up airline. Air Bahama, once flying, was due to start a Luxembourg to Bahama route, with a stop at Shannon. It was the Shannon connection, plus Aer Lingus' reputation for in-flight service that, according to the President of Air Bahama, was the best in the world, that brought in the training contract. It was not to be the last, and over the next few decades, cabin crew from around the world would be brought to Dublin for their training. The Aer Lingus tradition of service and friendliness has, because of the airline's role as a teacher of others, spread far beyond its own cabins.

After the glamour associated with the early stewardesses, and the space and service that were part of the jumbo jet era, the nature of the cabin crew began to change rapidly during the 1970s. The first sign of changing attitudes came in 1970, when the rules on women employees who married were lifted. Whereas previously all women who chose to marry had to leave the airline, from 1970, they were allowed to stay on. While it was a positive change, it meant that a regular feature in the pages of the staff magazine *Aer Scéala* disappeared. Up to that date, nearly every issue of the magazine featured a woman from one of the airline's many departments being presented with her marriage gift from her colleagues. In many ways, until 1970, the gift was as much to mark the woman's departure as it was to celebrate her nuptials. The pace of change within the airline's thinking, or rather the outside world, was signified most spectacularly in 1977, when the Employment Equality Agency criticised the airline for running adverts for stewardesses. In law, this effectively meant that men were excluded, and the airline was in the wrong. Aer Lingus accepted the critique, and in June 1978, Michael Duncan, the first male member of cabin crew, started work on board.

Despite the wider societal changes in attitudes towards the women of Ireland, those women who worked in the Aer Lingus cabins were far from content. While the cabin crew, according to surveys undertaken in 1979 and 1980, were happy to represent the airline, they felt that they were undervalued by management and, most importantly, that they were underpaid. Most tellingly, given *The Irish Times* view of 1945 that the job of an Air Hostess was little more than looking after the customers, the respondents to the 1979 survey argued

Introducing the Aer Lingus Business Travel Desk

Aer Lingus 🍀

While seen by economy passengers as the pampered elite, business travellers remain a key component of the Aer Lingus business on its transatlantic flights. In the 1980s, the airline began developing a range of exclusive services, including a dedicated booking line, for its business travellers. Although the design looks dated now, the image of computerised booking services symbolised the cutting edge services on offer.

The uniforms for all Aer Lingus staff, but particularly cabin crew, have been regularly changed over the years, and a named Irish designer brought in to dream up something befitting the practical demands of the job and combining the trends of the era. The crew here sport the outdoor wear from the 1980s.

Over the decades there have been different versions of cabin crew uniforms (they are pictured here chronologically, working left to right). The second uniform, introduced in 1948, was the first to be green, and this was replaced a decade later by the first uniform to be designed by a couturier, namely Irene Gilbert. The 1963 uniform was designed by Nelli Mulchahy, which in turn was replaced three years later by the Irene Gilbert two-piece ivy green uniform and the return of the forage style cap. The 1970s mini skirted version of the uniform, by Digby Morton, was most famous for its accompanying green tights. The more practical and sober outfits of the 1980s onwards have outlasted their various predecessors, and the most recent version of the uniform was designed by Louise Kennedy.

that, as the job was so demanding, they should have a right to retire at forty-five years of age. The survey was carried out in response to a Federated Workers' of Ireland strike, across most of Aer Lingus, between March and May 1978. Cabin crew joined the strike, and despite its eventual resolution to the satisfaction of the union, there was a belief that the job, while still having appeal, was hard work and misunderstood by many who saw it as work for well-groomed women.

Such attitudes ignored the changing nature of flight, and the sheer number of routes that Aer Lingus were flying. Given the oil crisis in the 1970s, and the world recession of the early 1980s, many airlines went out of business. The key for any airline was to get paying passengers on board, but at the same time reduce costs and prices. The very act of flying was being democratised, and in the process, the job of cabin crew shifted completely. With the advent of budget airlines, and the ending of complimentary drinks and food on board, so the role of cabin crew changed. Rather than being seen as the glamorous dispensers of care and service, they were seen on many airlines as people selling everything from food to scratch cards. As explained earlier, Aer Lingus took a diverse approach to its services during the 1990s. It preserved a multi-class service on its transatlantic services, but switched to a single economy class approach, given the nature of the competition and customer demand, on its British and European routes.

Nowadays cabin crew have a life that their counterparts from the 1940s would scarcely recognise. While core elements of the job remain, such as customer care and safety, the hours worked and the routes flown have changed dramatically. Rapid turnaround times for European flights, greater passenger numbers and a speed of service on board are the norm. All cabin crews are now mixed, and apart from a small band of very frequent fliers, it is doubtful that many passengers are known to the crew by name. Being a member of cabin crew is still a desirable job, but it is one that is hard work and comes with a great deal of responsibility. It is still glamorous, but perhaps not as much as it once was.

6 Passengers

In December 1964, Dublin airport played host to one of its many famous passengers. For the man in question, Cuban revolutionary leader Che Guevara, the arrival in Dublin was a surprise, as he was actually due to be flying to Algeria from New York. Fog in Shannon had meant that the brief Irish stopover was diverted to Dublin. Although not flying with Aer Lingus, the airline's staff played an integral part in his short stop in the country. Never ones to miss out on a story, RTÉ dispatched a reporter, Sean Egan, to the airport in the hope he might get an interview with the famous Argentinean. Egan was in luck as Guevara agreed, but the revolutionary had no English and the reporter no Spanish. Into the breach stepped Aer Lingus stewardess, Felima Archer, who sat in on the interview, still in her uniform, and translated between the two.

Sitting on board a plane, it is always interesting to speculate on who your fellow passengers are, and why they are flying on that particular day to their stated destination. Are they flying away on holiday, for business, to visit relatives or connecting onwards to travel even further? Given Ireland's history of emigration, we can also wonder whether these people are flying away for a new life somewhere else in the world. Over the decades, Aer Lingus has carried millions of passengers. Some have been famous, most of them not, and in non-human form they have carried everything from family pets to thoroughbred racehorses. For many, the plane is simply a way of getting from one place to the next, but for many more, sitting on board an Aer Lingus plane has been part of an Irish experience. Whether as tourists flying into Ireland for a holiday, and wanting an Irish airline, or for a native returning home, the green shamrock

For the elite few arriving at Baldonnel, in 1936, for Aer Lingus' first flight, the facilities for them to use were rudimentary. This ramshackle looking building was actually the 'lounge' for passengers waiting to board their planes. No wonder that the move to Desmond FitzGerald's terminal building, at Collinstown, was met with such enthusiasm.

tailfin, and the Irish accents on board, have been an important part of the Aer Lingus journey. For others like Che Guevara, who never even intended to interact with Aer Lingus, there was, when he needed a translator, an Aer Lingus stewardess to help him out.

Long before Che Guevara landed in Dublin, by which time plane travel had become more of an everyday experience, Aer Lingus attracted only two fare-paying passengers onto its inaugural flight (the other three passengers were all attached to the airline and did not hand over any money). It is not clear why Mr and Mrs T. Fitzherbert chose to avail of the new service, although their final destination was London, but it was probably their friendship with W. H. Morton, a director of both Great Southern Railways and Aer Lingus, that led them to be on board. The airline's chairman, Seán Ó hUadhaigh, was keen to avoid any negative publicity surrounding the first flight, and was relieved to hear from his wife that the Fitzherberts, although fifty-five minutes late into Bristol, and missing their train connection, were quite pleased with the flight. For the millions who came after the Fitzherberts, we know little about why many of them chose to travel with Aer Lingus, but given the loyalty to the airline of many of the passengers over the years, we have to presume, that like the Fitzherberts, they were quite pleased with what they experienced.

The background of the Fitzherberts does tell us something about the kinds of passengers flying in the early years. Mrs Fitzherbert was the daughter of Joseph Xavier Murphy, former TD and Governor of the Bank of Ireland, and at the time his daughter flew, he was a director of the Bank of Ireland, Guardian Insurance, Great Southern Railways and the Dublin Alliance and Consumer's Gas Council. Basically, they were a well off and influential family in Dublin circles. The Fitzherberts were just the kind of people who needed to, and could afford to take to the skies in the 1930s.

When Aer Lingus began growing its routes after the Second World War, passengers were initially few and far between. While the airline strove to drive down costs so that it could compete with ferry and railway companies into Britain, there was still a lingering perception that flying was for the wealthy. In the 1950s, the airline relied on a diet of regular fliers, mostly business people,

My first trip with Aer Lingus was as a 'nipper' in the early 1970s, travelling from Dublin to Shannon on a class tour, and we all looked forward to our first flight in an Aer Lingus 747 jumbo jet. We departed from the now iconic 'old terminal building' and walked out to the aircraft and could not believe our eyes. We were all mesmerised by the sheer size of the aircraft which had the biggest green shamrock we had ever seen — matched only by the biggest smiles of the cabin crew welcoming us aboard the flight. As the jumbo took off at Dublin we all felt like astronauts riveted to our seats as the aircraft sped down the runway and then lifted gracefully off the ground.

Joe Mulvaney, Cargo Operations

who plied their trade between Ireland and Britain. Such was the regularity of many of the passengers that they became known in person to the stewardesses. As Maree Sheehy, one of the earlier Aer Lingus stewardesses recalled, 'you got to know your passengers very well. One way or another their names were discovered en route. You were very disappointed if by the end of the flight you couldn't use all their names when you said goodbye.' Such memories speak to the personal service that early passengers received, but were also a result of the comparatively low passenger numbers. In the 1950s, most planes in the Aer Lingus fleet carried fewer than forty passengers when fully booked. With an hour or two in the air, on a half booked flight, it is perhaps unsurprising that passengers were known by name.

While most people who flew in the early days were regulars and known to the staff, even new faces became quickly known. As Maureen White, who worked for Flight Services in the late 1940s, pointed out, flights to London often lasted more than two hours, more than enough time to introduce oneself to a score of passengers. With the expansion of Aer Lingus routes into Europe, and from 1958, across the Atlantic, the type of passengers began to change. Rather than a small band of regulars who traversed the routes between Dublin and Britain, more infrequent and one-off passengers emerged.

A frequent flier on Aer Lingus, given his position as head of the government, Eamon de Valera is pictured here leaving a plane having flown from Dublin to Shannon. He was not the first, and every successive Taoiseach would use the airline for their official state business.

Irish screen legend Maureen O'Hara was closely linked to aviation as her husband had flown the last sea plane out of Foynes, and the first passenger land plane to touch down at Shannon. With the sea planes gone, Maureen O'Hara became a great supporter of Aer Lingus, and is shown here in 1960, at the Philadelphia office, after making a reservation.

In the late 1950s and early 1960s, there were two main types of airline passenger who seemed to dominate the lists of those on board. The first were business passengers who continued to fly into London and other major European cities for work (and these included everyone from high financiers to cattle traders), and second, a group who were the product of a stunted Irish economy: the emigrants. In the 1950s, Ireland's economy was in the doldrums. Outward emigration figures in that decade regularly amounted to 20,000 per year, and many chose to leave the country by air. While Seán Lemass could have never envisaged his dream of a national airline being used to transport the young people of the country to foreign shores, this sadly became a core of Aer Lingus' business. In 1961, just three years after Aer Lingus had begun flying the Atlantic, the United States television channel, CBS, made a documentary about contemporary Ireland. Titled *The Tear and the Smile,* the documentary was in part an examination of Ireland's move away from isolationism and its embrace of industrial modernity, but it also examined the human cost of the moribund economy. In one scene, Shannon is depicted as a modern airport linking Ireland to the United States, yet many of those boarding a transatlantic flight were being seen off by tearful relatives. These were not young Irish people in search of a short adventure or holiday, but rather were those who had chosen to seek better prospects over the seas. The Irish government criticised the programme for its negative portrayal of Ireland, but the black-and-white images paint a stark reality. Irish emigrants from the late 1950s, bound for the United States, did not cross the Atlantic in ship's steerage, but rather they sat in Aer Lingus' economy class. Unwittingly, the airline, which would pride itself on its wealth creation for the nation, was making some of its income as the vehicle for exporting the nation's people. The ritual of emigrating by plane, which has never really been written about, was a mainstay of the 1950s, the 1980s and again in the 2010s. Whereas the nineteenth century had stories of deprivation and death aboard the coffin ships, the twentieth-century emigrant experience was one of an eight-hour flight to the east coast of the United States, an on-board movie and whatever meal was served. It is not the stuff of great literature, but a departing that was shared by hundreds of thousands of people who left Ireland on board an Aer Lingus plane.

My most memorable experience was being part of the crew on the flight that the first baby ever was born aboard an Aer Lingus aircraft, in dramatic circumstances. The flight was from Beira, Mozambique to Lisbon in Portugal, via Luanda in Angola. The baby was born at 15,000 feet on Wednesday, 11 June 1975 at 18.35 GMT over Zambia, west of Lusaka. The Boeing 747 was on charter for the flight to TAP, the Portuguese Airline in June 1975. Cabin crew members on board the jumbo christened the baby Patrick. The name of the aircraft was St Patrick. There were three pilots and sixteen hostesses, all Irish, on board.

Maria Murphy, Retired, Flight Services

Compared to the misery of emigration, another of Aer Lingus' key routes from 1954 was the potentially uplifting pilgrimage flight to Lourdes. Catholic Ireland had long identified Lourdes, and its healing properties, as a key site of pilgrimage. The airline understood this, and began offering a range of flights, which were heavily marketed, so that people could visit. Planes were adapted so that the disabled and sick could be flown in comfort, and even the airline staff involved themselves with an annual fund-raising drive to ensure some less well off passengers could benefit from time spent in Lourdes. The opening of the Lourdes route in 1954 was suggested by Garret FitzGerald, and was timed to coincide with the centenary of the shrine. That year alone there were eighty-two planes of pilgrims flown to the French town, and while underpinned by a religious sensitivity within the state airline, it also proved to be good business. In addition to pilgrims, Aer Lingus plied a steady trade in flying members of religious orders. Until the 1970s, the Irish Catholic Church was highly active overseas, and there was a constant traffic of priests and nuns travelling to meetings, away to work as missionaries or else moving to new parishes abroad. As a result, one of the most frequent shots taken by the Dublin airport photographer in the 1950s and 1960s, were various priests and nuns ascending the stairs of an Aer Lingus plane en route to variety of religious sites and gatherings.

AERSCEALA

STOP PRESS
OCTOBER 1951

Children, depending where you are sitting and how noisy they are, can be either the most delightful companions on a flight or the worst. Today, strict rules govern the age of unaccompanied children boarding an aircraft. This was not always the case, and many a hostess spent their flight caring for young charges, such as this boy disembarking in London.

Early planes, for all the interest in them and the fascination with the technology and the glamour, were actually cramped and noisy affairs. In the early 1950s, the total number of passengers on any of Aer Lingus' planes were much smaller than they are now. So while the passengers got tray, and not trolley service, they were more cramped, their flights took longer and their ears took a bashing.

One of the most common features in *Aer Scéala* was the page that featured the comings and goings of the rich and famous on Aer Lingus flights. In this issue from 1964, the pop fans got to see Cliff Richard chatting with Pauline Guerin and Grace Cross, while for the followers of American political life, there was the arrival into Dublin of Mrs Edward Kennedy, with her sister Candice McMurray, being greeted by the then Minister for Agriculture, Charles Haughey.

Of all the great music acts in the history of the world, the Beatles remain the most significant and recognisable. In the mid-1960s, when they were at the height of their fame, they travelled to Dublin on an Aer Lingus flight, to play a concert in Ireland. Met by a large crowd of fans and the press, the Fab Four spent their time after disembarkation playing up for the cameras.

In addition to specific routes that catered for a defined need, such as pilgrims to Lourdes, Aer Lingus was, by the 1960s and 1970s, flying to a wide range of European cities. These routes were heavily marketed by the airline to ensure a good rate of inbound passengers (tourists to Ireland) and outbound ones (tourists going overseas). In this publicity they were assisted by RTÉ. During that period one of its most successful radio presenters was Harry Thuillier. He used his own production house to make a variety of light entertainment programmes. One of his most successful and enduring, which he made with the assistance of Aer Lingus, was called *Come Fly with Me*. The signature tune was Frank Sinatra's famous recording. Thuillier's stroke of genius was that he tied in with the airline, and he would fly wherever an Aer Lingus plane was going on a particular day, be it Rome or Paris or Berlin. Thuillier would take his small tape recorder and chat with the passengers and find out who they were and what they were doing. At that time, flying was very exotic. Only a small group of people could afford to do it. These tapes would be sent back to RTÉ, and turned into programmes. This was really exotic to the Irish listener at that time, and every programme began with his announcement that, 'Here I am in Barcelona', or wherever he had chosen to go. Thuillier was part of a wave of publicity, albeit one of the most popular, that was encouraging Irish people to travel by air. Radio shows, newspaper and magazine articles and word of mouth were all encouraging Irish people to take to the air and to travel. Passengers were no longer the business hacks who had to be in London by 9 o'clock in the morning, but were also the couple or the family who decided that they wanted to see Paris, Berlin or Rome for themselves.

Since the 1960s, many of Aer Lingus' passengers have been tourists. A good many of these, as will be discussed in the final chapter, were tourists who were travelling to Ireland on holiday, especially from the United States. For those leaving Ireland on holiday, Aer Lingus began with short routes to traditional British holiday resorts such as Blackpool and the Isle of Man, but over the years passenger demand led to a more varied diet. In the 1960s and 1970s, holidays in Spanish and Mediterranean resorts became more common, and many of the airline's passengers were families, couples and groups travelling for two weeks of fun in the sun. These were both on scheduled flights, and also on the airline's own Spanish charter service. By 1980, passengers responding to a survey enquiring about their reasons for travel on Aer Lingus made clear how important tourism had become, with 65 per cent of those flying on European routes, and 88 per cent on the transatlantic route, travelling for leisure.

The tourists were the key component of the passengers on board. While Aer Lingus has always flown to and promoted skiing resorts, the boom in winter sports holidays has been a phenomenon of the last decade or so. In part this reflected a switch in people's interests, but it was also the product of increased wealth in the Irish economy. Whereas previously people were choosing a single holiday during the year, from the mid-1990s, many families were able to have a mixed vacation diet that might encompass a sun holiday and a winter sports break, as well as short weekends away in major European cities or else attending sporting events. All these different options meant that an ever increasing number of passengers were boarding Aer Lingus flights, and heading to a variety of different destinations. This marked an important shift in the way people thought about flying. Rather than the plane ride being an integral part of the vacation experience, a once-yearly happening, it became a frequent occurrence, and the flight no longer seemed part of the adventure. A great boost for the wallets of passengers was the switch, by Aer Lingus, to a low fares model on its European routes in the early 2000s. Lower fares enabled more passengers to get more places, and suddenly the idea of a

Opposite top: Once planes are called in departures and boarding commences, all passengers are ready to take their seat and fly. In the 1950s, Aer Lingus installed its new boarding desks at Dublin airport. The one carry on item for each passenger was as true then as it is today.

Opposite bottom: For the lucky few, especially with Aer Lingus' purchase of its first transatlantic Boeings, travelling first class was a luxurious joy. In the Golden Shamrock first class service, passengers had room to move around, their own seats and their own lounge area for sharing drinks. The lounge was decorated with stylised maps of Ireland, completed by the crests of the four provinces and, back in the day, smoking was allowed.

1962 IRISH SWEEPS DERBY

TO BE RUN IN **IRELAND** ON JUNE 30

ESTIMATED PRIZE MONEY

£60,000

ONE OF THE WORLD'S RICHEST RACES!

Fly AER LINGUS
IRISH INTERNATIONAL AIRLINES

PRINTED IN THE REPUBLIC OF IRELAND BY CAHILL & CO. LTD. PARKGATE PRINTING WORKS DUBLIN.

weekend in Barcelona was not the stuff of luxury, but an affordable and attainable goal.

The last decade or so saw a rapid growth of Aer Lingus routes into the eastern European nations. Here a new passenger base was found. Not only were Irish people beginning to experience new cities and new countries, but with the Celtic Tiger boom coinciding with the expansion of the European Union in 2004, so Ireland welcomed workers from Poland, Latvia, Lithuania and other places. These young men and women, leaving home to find work in Ireland, were not only the nation's first major wave of immigrants, but they were also a new cohort of passengers for the airline.

Of all the millions who have flown Aer Lingus, it is the VIPs that we all see in the newspapers. As the national airline flying in and out of Ireland, Aer Lingus has brought many famous people to their destination. The former staff magazine, *Aer Scéala,* as well as the national media, has captured the comings and goings of the rich and famous on various Aer Lingus flights. Whatever their fame, all these people were passengers, and they have included an array of pop stars, movie celebrities, politicians, beauty queens and sports stars. Amongst its many important passengers, sports teams have been regulars on board. Aer Lingus has frequently flown the Irish national rugby and soccer teams overseas, and was chosen as the airline to take the first ever touring GAA side to Australia. For that touring Meath team of 1967, the decision of Aer Lingus to proudly carry the team was a great boost, as they had to raise the money for the tour themselves. The only problem was that Aer Lingus only flew as far as Rome, so the Meath team had to then make a series of

One of the great gambling phenomena of twentieth-century Irish life, in the days before the lotto, was the Irish sweepstake. Played by people across the globe, who bought tickets for a chance to win a fortune, the sweepstake linked the idea of a raffle with major horse races from the Irish calendar. Such was the interest in the sweepstake, that many wanted to visit Ireland to attend the races, a marketing opportunity that Aer Lingus did not let pass by.

connecting flights onwards with other airlines. The links between the airline and sport were cemented from 1966, when it flew the Celtic soccer team for a European match in Tiblisi. From then until the mid-1980s, Aer Lingus was a key carrier of English and Scottish club sides for their European fixtures. Most famously, the airline flew the Liverpool squad back from Rome after it had won the European Cup in 1977, and the British press was left with the incongruous image of the team captain, Emlyn Hughes, descending the stairs with the trophy from an Aer Lingus plane.

The airline has carried all the major officials of the Irish government over the decades, from every Taoiseach since Eamon de Valera, as well as the successive Presidents since Seán T. O'Kelly. Perhaps more beautiful than the politicians, but no less important to the history of the state, were the competitors in the Rose of Tralee competition, which the airline has a long connection with. Indeed, two former Roses were Aer Lingus employees: the 1959 Rose, Alice O'Sullivan, and the 1991 winner, Denise Murphy. Possibly cuter than the Roses, the airline has also been responsible for flying various animals into Ireland that were destined for Dublin Zoo. Famously, these included, on 12 June 1986, two giant pandas, Ming Ming and Ping Ping.

In the battle to decide Aer Lingus' most famous passengers, the choice perhaps comes down to two. The first claimed to be bigger than Jesus, and the second could be said to be closest to him. On 7 November 1963, the Beatles flew into Dublin on board an Aer Lingus flight to perform at the city's Adelphi Cinema. This was the only time that the band ever played in Ireland, and on arrival they were swamped by fans who had sat at the airport awaiting their arrival. A quarter of a century later, on 29 September 1979, Pope

For many people nowadays a sun holiday means just that: guaranteed sunshine in the Canaries or on a Mediterranean beach. In the 1960s, such luxurious destinations, while becoming available to greater numbers, were still out of the reach of many. For lots of families, their sun holiday meant flying with Aer Lingus to the Tower and Golden Mile of Blackpool.

fáilte romat

welcome aboard

Your flight is about to begin. Perhaps by the time you read these words, it may have begun. To our experienced crew, this is yet another trip over a familiar route. In one important respect, however, this flight differs from all others: you and your fellow passengers are unique, each and everyone requiring special and individual attention. It will be our aim to provide it throughout the journey.

Prior to the advent of in-flight magazines, passengers were presented with a booklet of information. This included details of how the overhead lights and air worked, safety information and here, from the early 1960s, a welcome for all the sartorially elegant passengers.

John Paul II arrived in Dublin on board the Boeing 747, St Patrick. It was a key event for Ireland, but also for the airline. This was the first time that a Pope had flown out of Italy on any airline other than Alitalia. The plane, with fourteen cabin crew on board, was specially converted for Papal use, and decorated with the Papal insignia alongside the livery of Aer Lingus. It was piloted by Captain Thomas McKeown, who had joined the airline back in 1945. While in Ireland, the Pope was ferried between towns and cities on board the Aer Lingus-owned Irish Helicopters. When he left Ireland, on 1 October, bound for Boston, he again flew the Irish airline. While many now view the visit of Pope John Paul II as a high-water mark for Catholic Ireland, it was undoubtedly the most significant service that the airline has ever provided for a passenger.

In 2009, Aer Lingus carried nearly 40 per cent of all passengers entering Irish airports. While the concept of service has changed over the decades, and our expectations of our on-board experience have shifted, passengers remain the key driving force in Aer Lingus' business. Currently, just over 80 per cent of the airline's revenue is derived from passenger fares. Each and every day, passengers board an Aer Lingus plane, flying off in various directions for different reasons, and each one of them will have a tale to tell. ✈

159

Top: Of the many sports teams that have flown Aer Lingus, many were not even Irish. Landing here at Dublin airport, were members of the Scottish rugby team of 1962, scheduled to play the Irish at Lansdowne Road.

Bottom: Of all the regular fliers on Aer Lingus during the 1950s, 60s and 70s, members of the religious were very frequent. Whether flying for pilgrimage, off to missionary work, or away to new postings, the sight of priests and nuns on planes was not unusual. These Franciscan nuns, being greeted by Nuala Doyle of the airline, were travelling from the United States into Ireland.

Top: Flights to Lourdes, from 1958, were a boon to the Aer Lingus business. The Catholic Irish were keen consumers of the Lourdes pilgrimage, and this flight, in 1962, was one of the sixty-plus flights that left to Lourdes every summer.

Bottom: Emigrants formed a regular component of Aer Lingus' business. Whether moving to the United States or Britain, flights during recession years were constantly packed with those choosing to leave Ireland. In 1961, Mrs Mary Murtagh, accompanied by her six children, and seen off by ground hostess, Anne Flynn, had decided to leave Ireland for a new life in the United States.

Outside of Pope John Paul II, in 1979, the most significant and publicly acclaimed international figure to have visited Ireland was the President of the United States, John F. Kennedy. He arrived in Ireland in 1963 for a four day visit, and although flying, as all President's do, on Airforce One, Aer Lingus ensured that the steps he descended down were theirs. These images were flashed around Ireland and the United States, and the whole visit ensured a boom in American visitors to Ireland in the succeeding years.

Entertaining children on board has always been a challenge for airlines. While it is now easier, given the range of entertainments on offer, it was not always so. In trying to encourage children to think about the different flights they took, and to see themselves as potential pilots, Aer Lingus introduced the Passenger Log Book for children in the 1980s. On each flight they could complete details of where they had flown, on what kind of plane and a host of other details, as a way of passing the time (*courtesy of Kay O'Rourke*).

The arrival of Pope John Paul II, at Dublin airport, on 29 September 1979, was a moment of huge significance for Ireland and Aer Lingus. The moment when he appeared at the door of his flight, cheered on by thousands and live on Irish television, was one of the proudest for the staff of the airline.

Aer Lingus' most important passenger, Pope John Paul II, is seen here, studying his script for his speech on arrival in Dublin, on board the Boeing 747, St Patrick.

Arriving at the airport, checking in, waiting around. Sometimes it can all get too much for some passengers, and the only option is to sleep. In July 1962, one young Aer Lingus passenger decided that, despite the attractions of the airport, the best thing to do was to sleep until the plane was ready.

7 On Board

Flying from one place to another necessitates time

spent on board a plane. An hour or so flying from Dublin to Heathrow can pass quickly, whereas seven or more hours spent flying to Boston, Chicago or New York can drag. Much of this depends on what happens on board. Delays are an unfortunate reality for anyone flying, but the time spent in the cabin can fly by dependant on the quality of two big issues that have always been at the forefront of passengers' minds: food and entertainment. There are always those self-sufficient travellers who are happy to stick their nose into a book, put on their headphones and lose themselves in their music, do some work or simply go to sleep. For the rest of us, especially on longer flights, we expect the airline to keep us happy.

Pre-war fliers on Aer Lingus got their seat on board, and little else. The concept of in-flight service was restricted by the small size of the plane, the lack of a galley and, until 1945, the lack of any cabin crew to serve anything. It was the arrival of the cabin crew, and the purchasing of ever larger and more modern planes, that really shifted Aer Lingus, and other airlines, from a seat-only operation, to what they have become nowadays: airborne entertainment systems, shops in the sky and restaurants on the wing.

A 1951 edition of *Aer Scéala* focused on what it called 'cabin service'. The new generation of planes purchased by Aer Lingus after the war meant that on-board service had become a reality. Also of great significance was the opening of Dublin airport. The airport gained an excellent reputation as a place to eat, and people travelled from the surrounding area to dine there while watching the planes taxi and take off. One British newspaper, in the late 1950s, even gave the airport restaurant the title of serving 'the best airport food in the world'. In those early days of on-board catering, it was the airport restaurant and catering staff that provided the meals for the planes. What was excellent on the ground was expected to be the same quality in the air. Writing in *Aer Scéala*, J. K. Emm outlined the varied needs of passengers in the early 1950s:

> There is the passenger who feels cold and needs a rug; another who is tired and wants a head rest pillow; an active fellow who has to write a few business letters; an avid reader who demands a variety of newspapers and magazines; the bloke who is interested in the panorama down below and needs a map to follow the track. Then there are ordinary passengers like you and I who are contented with a bite to eat, a few cups of coffee or a glass or two of the best to sustain the inner man until Aer Lingus ushers us out of our comfortable seats at the end of the flight.

Food for this array of passengers was prepared, for outbound aircraft, at either Dublin or Shannon airport. At first these were simple sandwiches, but by the 1950s, with the increase in galley size, hot dishes such as soup were added. One early innovation made by Aer Lingus was to offer a variety of goods for sale on its planes. These included cigarettes, chocolates, wines and spirits. Such was the novelty of being able to buy such products in post-Emergency Ireland (and at duty free rates) that the airline did a sterling business. In the winter months of 1950, on-board sales brought in £1,500 per month, and this grew to over £3,000 in August. For an airline establishing its business and trying to push itself to profitability, on-board sales were an important boost to revenue.

By the late 1950s, the Atlantic had opened up for Aer Lingus, and a whole rethinking of on-board services was required. Passengers were no longer on board for a couple of hours, but would have to be fed, watered and entertained for perhaps ten hours, including refuelling stops in Gander in northeastern Newfoundland, Canada and elsewhere. The delivery of the airline's first Boeing

aerlingus, ceóranca.
aerport áca cliac, baile domnaill. 1789
DUBLIN AIRPORT, BALDONNEL.

	uimir (Number) Seirbis (Service)	Dáca (Date)

ainm (Name) MR BREWSTER
ó (From) CROYDON
go (To) DUBLIN   luac (Fare) £1 10 0
áiceanna cúirlingce ar ar aoncuigeao bristol
(Agreed Stopping Places)   maic go ocí
(Valid until) 28·5·37
cugca amac ag LH   Dáca a cugca amac.   ticéad bagáiste uimir
(Issued by)   (Date of Issue)   (Baggage Ticket No.)
(At) Dublin   25·5·37
Fá na coingeallaca iomcárca lascall.
(Subject to Conditions of Carriage on Back).

Original airline tickets were rudimentary affairs. Rather than a neat electronic print out, Aer Lingus relied on tickets that were handwritten for each individual passenger. In May 1937, a Mr Brewster flew from Dublin to Croydon airport, London, and paid one pound and ten shillings for his seat.

Baggage labels are there for a purpose, in that they help us identify which bags are ours. Long before the bar code linked bags to individuals, many airlines, Aer Lingus included, made adhesive baggage labels available to its customers. The airline used these labels to visually represent itself, and in the 1950s, the stylised shamrock was a recognisable image on bags across Europe.

To me Aer Lingus is more than another airline. It is an expression of the Irish nation and character. In the same way as St Patrick's Day, Guinness, U2 and many others, we in Aer Lingus are ambassadors for our country. For a small airline we have a large presence in world aviation.

Jonathan Morgan, Cabin Operations

planes signalled another new departure: first class travel. Things that we now take for granted, such as a diet of films and television programmes, did not come on board until the era of the jumbo jet in the early 1970s. The trick, during the 1960s, seems to have been over-feeding everyone! Food was provided on a regular basis, and every meal was a full one – there were no snacks on the early transatlantic route. For first class travellers, there was a lounge area where board games, newspapers and magazines were provided to pass the time. Alcohol was freely available and smoking was allowed throughout the plane. With greater space, and bigger galleys on these flights, the range of items for sale grew beyond wines and spirits, and stretched to include a range of Irish goods. The Irish brand of Aer Lingus was an important component of on-board service. Crockery, glasses, cutlery and napkins were all sourced from Irish firms, so that each passenger, whether familiar with the brands or not, got to eat with, and off, the best that the country could offer.

From the 1970s, a shift took place in the provision of on-board services. While there was still a full bar on all services, the realisation was made that these were a source of earning potential. While everything in first class remained complimentary, the paid bar – served from a trolley, as the trays had been retired – made its entrance on transatlantic economy flights and across Europe. Looking through the pages of *Cara* magazine from the early 1980s, one is struck by how cheap everything seems. Cocktails – that is a range of spirits – were available for £1.30, and a can from a selection of beers cost a mere sixty pence. The range of products available on board had grown still further, and in those

173

days duty free goods were still available for passengers flying within Europe. Offerings from the on-board shop in the early 1980s included Chanel No 5 at £21, Kouros aftershave for £11, Claddagh rings for £42, an Aer Lingus hostess doll for £5 and a video of *Ireland, the Isles of Memories* for £19. In addition to the shopping, planes now had on-board entertainment. At first, this was in the form of music fed through armrests, followed by the fitting of single screens to each cabin section. While this meant that everyone had to watch the same programming, at the same time, it was a revelation for many passengers. In September 1986, for instance, transatlantic passengers were able to enjoy two films outbound from Ireland, *Million Dollar Mystery* (starring Tom Bosley), described as 'an entertaining comedy', and *Sweet Lorraine* (starring Maureen Stapleton and Trini Alvarado), which was billed as 'a well crafted movie'. Once the films were finished, or in their place for passengers who did not wish to watch, there were eight channels of music which featured classical, country, rock n' roll, an entire Elvis Presley channel and four Irish music channels. These included 'The Dubliners … A Celebration' and 'Paddy Reilly's Ireland'. That there was only one channel of contemporary chart music, compared to the four featuring traditional Irish music, speaks volumes about the expected clientele on board: they were likely to be older, and as the key market at that time was American tourists, more interested in things Irish, than modern pop music.

With the switch to Airbus for the transatlantic routes, facilities on board changed once more. The current generation of individual screens for each passenger were installed, and a rich diet of entertainment fed to all. Nowadays, passengers travelling to and from the United States with Aer Lingus can enjoy nine film channels, which begin on demand. There are a multitude of television and music channels, and a series of computer games to keep young and old amused. Food on board, which was being criticised across the airline industry by the 1980s for the constant diet of poor quality 'rubber chicken', was updated on all Aer Lingus flights. By the mid-1990s and into the 2000s, the arrival of budget airlines had reshaped how Aer Lingus flew across Europe. As a single economy class airline, with short flights and quick turnaround times, the decision was made to provide passengers with a range of food and drink for

In 1960, as Aer Lingus readied itself to take delivery of its first jet planes, *Aer Scéala* ran a series of articles for the staff titled, 'Preparing for Jets'. In one such column, in October 1960, the food available for first class passengers was highlighted. As the text informed the reader: 'de-luxe catering will be one of the selling attractions of our Boeing ... passengers will be offered cigarettes, a choice of champagne or cocktails, and dinner will consist of Hors d'Oeuvres, Soup, Fish, Joint, Vegetables, Salad, Dessert, Cheese, Petits Fours, Fruit, and Coffee, Tea or Irish Coffee, Wines and Liqueurs'.

The post-war years witnessed a rise in the numbers of Aer Lingus passengers, and also their expectations of on-board facilities and care. Here, a stewardess distributes newspapers, an early marker of in-flight service, to passengers.

Whatever the sumptuous services available on first class, on early transatlantic services, most passengers travelled economy. Stewardesses dispensed food to passengers, sitting three abreast, either side of the aisle, and the food, while not at the level of first class, was sumptuous by today's standards.

coming Back from Jersey.

AER LINGUS ✦ IRISH AIR LINES
Friendship Flight Report

Friendship Airliner St. *Shannon*　　　　**Date** 16·7·61
Eitleán Friendship N.　　　　　　　　　　　　　Dáta

proceeding to *Dublin*　　　　　　　　**at a speed of**
ar eite chuig　　　　　　　　　　　　　　　　　ar luas
volant vers　　　　　　　　　　　　　　　　　à la vitesse de

280 **m.p.h. Our altitude is** *8,000*　　　　　**feet. We**
m.s.u. Táimíd ar airde　　　　　　　　　　troigh. Thíos
miles à l'heure. Notre altitud e estde　　pieds. Nous

are now passing over *Irish Sea*　　　　　　　**Left**
fúinn anois tá　　　　　　　　　　　　　　　　　Ar chlé
survolons en ce moment　　　　　　　　　　À gauche

we may see *Holyhead*　　　　　　**at** *12·30* **hrs.**
uainn beidh　　　　　　　　　　　　　　　　　or
nous apercevrons　　　　　　　　　　　　　　u/ch.
　　　　　　　　　　　　　　　　　　　　　　heures.

Right we may see
Ar dheis uainn beidh
À droite nous pourrons voir

at ——— **hrs.**　　　　　**The weather at our destination**
or　　　　u/ch.　　　　　　Tá an aimsir ag ar gceannchúrsa
à　　　　heures.　　　　　Le temps à notre destination

is *Cloudy*　　　　　　　　**We are due to arrive**
est　　　　　　　　　　　　　Ba cheart go sroichfimís
　　　　　　　　　　　　　　Nous comptons arriver

at *Dublin Airport*　　**at** *12·55* **hrs. local time.**
or　　　　　　　　　　　　or　　　　u/ch. ám ditióll
à　　　　　　　　　　　　à　　　　heures (heure locale)

Remarks　　*pic*
Nótaí
Remarques

Captain *Pendleton*
Captaen
Capitaine

Co-Pilot *Kennedy*
Comhphíolóit
Co-pilote

Hostesses *Miss Cleary*
Bán-alochtóir
Hostesses

⟶ PLEASE PASS TO OTHER PASSENGERS

CUIR AR AGHAIDH CHUIG PAISINÉIRÍ EILE, LED THOIL　　　PRIÈRE DE FAIRE CIRCULER

1828/a-500Pds.(c)-9/59.

'Good morning ladies and gentlemen, this is the captain speaking...' Words that are familiar to anyone who has flown, and a signal that the plane is about to move from the stand. Prior to the development of on-board announcements, and given the high levels of cabin noise, more rudimentary means were used to communicate with the passengers. This Friendship Flight Report, from 1961, details the weather and expected flying times on a trip from Jersey to Dublin, and lists the crew. The scales of economy meant that there was only one such report, and passengers were asked at the base of the page 'Please pass to other passengers' (*courtesy of David Lavelle*).

purchase. This has led the airline to partner with various food companies and well-known chefs, to produce a range of sandwiches and snacks that have wide appeal through their use of well-known brands and ingredients. The ending of on-board duty free sales in European skies has meant the passage of wines, spirits and cigarettes as something to buy on board, but has also freed up galley and storage space, and led the airline to innovate in the range of goods that it sells. The airline's catering department refashioned its service for the transatlantic routes in the early 1990s. By 1996, the catering department employed over 300 staff, and they produced some 7,000 trays of food every day. As well as the standard dishes for economy passengers, the airline prided itself on, and won awards for, its first/business class service. By the mid–1990s, this would feature poached salmon and strawberries to start, a choice between a sole mousse or a fillet mignon, followed by a selection of desserts. All of this was washed down with a range of wines and spirits, and tea or coffee. In addition, the airline also has to cater for a wide variety of specialised diets, including vegetarian, Kosher, celiac, dairy free, diabetic and low cholesterol.

Clearly the flying experience has changed, and will continue to do so. Decades ago, the thought of having to amuse children on board a flight lasting several hours must have filled many a parent with fear. Today, the children on board, as well as all the other passengers flying the Atlantic routes of Aer Lingus, can chose from a dizzying array of entertainment choices, and be happily fed and watered. As ticket cost is the issue for passengers in Europe, most understand why what is now offered on board by the airline has changed. Our expectations for short haul are different, and economy is the key watchword. As the flag carrier for Ireland, Aer Lingus also concentrates heavily on standards. Its belief in a multi-class service on its transatlantic services, and the switch to a single economy class approach, given the nature of the competition and customer demand, on its British and European routes, means that the airline is giving its various passengers what they want, while still making the on-board experience an engaging, comfortable and enjoyable one. ✈

Aer Lingus always marketed the modernity of its fleet alongside its destinations, and given the fascination with the very idea of flight, posters exploring the construction and layout of planes, such as this for the Viscount, were a regular part of the Aer Lingus promotional arsenal.

As part of a United States wide advertising campaign in the 1960s, Aer Lingus ran this advertisement in a variety of publications. The focus was on economy class crossings, but stressed two important values at the heart of the airline's mission: quality of service and price.

There are two things that every passenger has to keep safe, once they are checked in: their boarding pass and their passport. This boarding pass, from the 1960s, was for flight EI650 from Dublin to Frankfurt. Note how the company name has, by this point, been standardised as Aer Lingus Irish. The same design of wording and the encircled shamrock were also used on the outside of the planes (*courtesy of Angela Marum*).

These days most of us print off our own tickets, to speed our way through the airport. Previously, all passengers were issued, either by the airline or a travel agent, a ticket, from which was torn a carbon copy for each leg that was flown. This ticket, from the 1960s, emphasises the Irishness of the airline in its bold use of green, and the ever present shamrock (*courtesy of Tom Plunkett*).

Opposite: The one constant message on all planes today is that smoking is strictly prohibited. This was not always the case, and airlines such as Aer Lingus readily partnered with tobacco companies to market their brands. Gold Flake was one such company, but there were many others who worked to promote smoking on board.

Above: Flying first class, on Aer Lingus' transatlantic flights, was incredibly expensive. While the airline gained huge credit for the excellence of its service, it remained the choice of the few. For those able to afford their seat in first class, an excellent range of food and drink was available, all served on the best Irish tableware.

Top: First class service was, and remains, unrecognisable from what happens in economy. The range of choice is greater, the food more beautifully presented, the seats bigger and even the blankets thicker. That said, for something that cost perhaps ten times as much as an economy ticket, the chance, as these passenger had in 1963, to choose your own particular type of pastry, was money well spent.

Bottom: Every day since Aer Lingus began serving food on its planes, the airline or its agents have made thousands of meals every day. This picture from the tray assembly line of the flight kitchen, in October 1978, demonstrates the size and scale of the operation that was undertaken to feed all the hungry mouths on board.

Life Jackets

You will find an inflatable life jacket of the latest design under your seat.

Please do not look at it now; it has been sealed for its own protection after its periodic inspection.

It can, however, be reached in a moment if required.

The picture sequence below shows you how to don and secure your jacket.

DO NOT INFLATE YOUR LIFE JACKET UNTIL YOU HAVE LEFT THE AIRCRAFT.

1. Pull life jacket over the head with lamp and valve on outside.

2. Pass tape around waist.

3. Tie tapes securely under jacket, at front.

4. AFTER LEAVING THE AIRCRAFT

Inflate by pulling smartly on the red operating knob. Inflation can also be done by blowing into the mouth-piece. To operate the light, insert plug into the socket of the battery. A whistle is also provided.

Printed in the Republic of Ireland by The Ormond Printing Co. Ltd.

40

The use of on-board videos to demonstrate on-board safety have been a feature of airline travel since the 1980s, and the plastic covered safety card a constant since the 1970s. In the 1960s, Aer Lingus presented its passengers with a booklet to explain such matters as how to inflate a life jacket.

The pages of the in-flight magazine, *Cara*, have been used as a way of advertising and displaying the vast array of goods that Aer Lingus has made available on its planes. This has included the staples of drinks and cigarettes, but also the novelty items associated with the airline. In 1986 fashions dictated that these included a Parker Pen, stewardess doll and lego kit so that the young flier could build their own planes.

8 Selling Ireland

In July 1938, the recently appointed General Manager of Aer Lingus, an American named Robert Logan who had been hired from Pan Am, wrote to the board of the airline with a suggestion. In a letter, which is now held in the archives of the Irish Railway Record Society, he wrote: 'in all parts of the world, with which I am familiar, there is a quick mental association of the shamrock with Ireland. While the Irish Harp appears to be the formal and official crest or emblem of Ireland, the shamrock seems to me to be the more popular commercial emblem, especially in foreign countries, and the chief purpose of our aircraft's insignia would be to display it to foreigners. In general, the shamrock should be in green with the initial letters of the company in white with the outline of the feathers in gold.' Although Logan would only remain in the job for a year, his vision of a shamrock on all Aer Lingus planes is his lasting legacy. Logan appeared a highly frustrated figure during his tenure as General Manager. He had come from a job in the United States where he was working for a rapidly expanding airline that flew many routes with a plethora of different planes. In Ireland, he found two planes and only short routes to Britain. Prior to his departure, due in part to the outbreak of the Second World War, Logan constantly demanded that the airline's board think big, and his vision for the shamrock is illustrative of his imagination. It was not enough for Aer Lingus to simply exist, and fly its small number of routes, rather that the airline should look to grow, and in the process mark itself out as specifically Irish. Logan, perhaps because of his knowledge of Irish America, knew full well the appeal, to many people, of the Irish identity. For him, if this sense of Irishness that many people identified with could be packaged up with the airline, then it would result in a clearer image of what Aer Lingus was – Ireland in the air – and this in turn would lead to greater visibility and recognition with the travelling public.

For Logan, and all his successors who have run the airline, promoting Aer Lingus and filling its planes was not their sole job. Aer Lingus also had a central role in selling Ireland as a destination. In an earlier chapter, the history of the routes out of Ireland were recounted, but as the national airline, and one in which the state has always had a large interest, it was the routes into Ireland that were the most significant. While outbound routes took people away, inbound routes brought travellers, and their wallets, to Ireland. As Ireland struggled, through much of the twentieth century, to prosper and develop industries that could create wealth for its people, tourism came to be seen as one of the most important parts of the economy. As a tourist destination, Ireland had much to offer. Not only was the country beautiful, but it had excellent fishing and golf facilities, a literary and musical heritage and an ancient history. While these features undoubtedly lured many people, the single biggest bonus Ireland had in developing a tourist industry was its diaspora. In North America particularly there were millions of people who claimed Irish descent, and would love to visit 'home'. After independence mass tourism into Ireland was not a feasible option. Not only did much of the country's infrastructure have to be rebuilt after years of war, but tourism was restricted to those of means and, given the time required to cross the Atlantic by ship, also required a degree of leisurely travelling.

The post-war years led to a real shift in thinking surrounding the potential for Irish tourism. The post-war boom in the United States meant that the numbers of tourists with the means to travel increased dramatically, and the opportunities afforded by the opening of transatlantic air routes – especially given Shannon's central place in such traffic – meant that passengers could travel to Ireland quickly and in large numbers. The need for Ireland to develop a tourism industry, and the government's desire to increase its foreign currency earnings, led to the publication of the Christenberry Report in 1951. This was the culmination of a number of mainly American reports that assessed what Ireland had to do to develop a successful tourist industry. The report

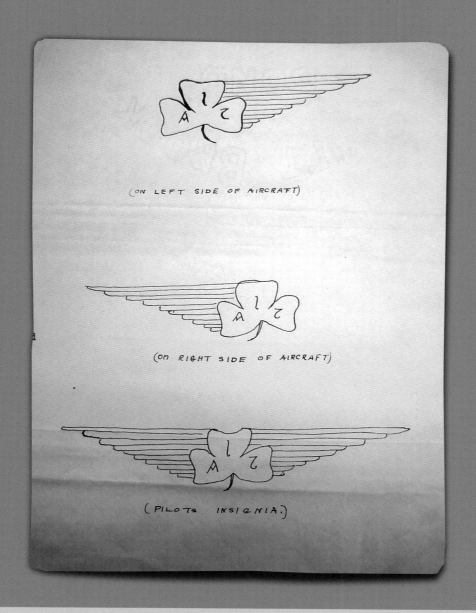

In 1938, the General Manager of Aer Lingus, Robert Logan, sketched these plans for the first Aer Lingus plane markings. He was keen to identify the airline as specifically Irish, and felt that the shamrock was the most readily recognised symbol available. Although supplanted by several successive designs of an Aer Lingus logo, the shamrock has remained a constant (*courtesy of the Irish Railway Record Society*).

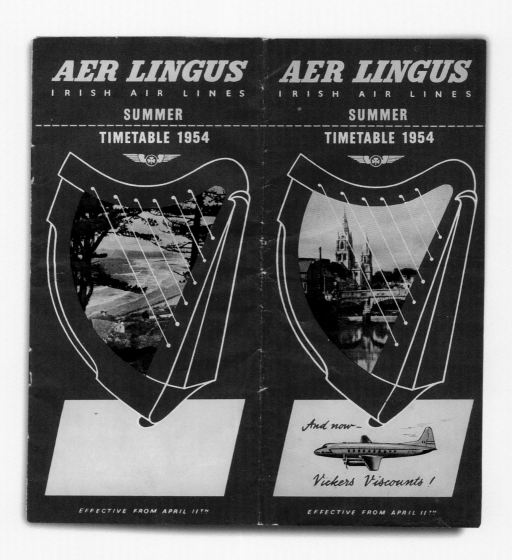

The Aer Lingus printed timetable has taken various forms over the decades, but were used on a regular basis to depict Irish scenes. This one from 1954 used the imagery of the Irish harp, interwoven with important sites that the visitor would want to visit (*courtesy of Tony Murray*).

dealt with everything from the expectation of visitors in terms of accommodation and dining (they would want hot showers, coffee and orange juice),
through to the types of things they might do (fishing, shooting and golf) and
the places they might visit (the counties of the western seaboard and the rural
west). Significantly, the report noted that when advertising the country as a
tourist destination, Ireland had to develop a clear sense of what it was. In the
same way that Logan had identified the shamrock as the logo for Aer Lingus,
so the country had to decide visually what it would be signified by. In time,
especially with the opening of the transatlantic route from 1958, Aer Lingus
would play a key role in selling Ireland.

Prior to the opening of the transatlantic route, and the realisation in
government from the early 1950s that tourism had the potential to be a big
business for Ireland, it was the British routes that were key to Aer Lingus in
boosting tourism. On flights in the first decade and a half of the airline's existence, passengers were regularly given leaflets extolling the virtues of Ireland
and the treasures that awaited them. Today this promotional literature looks
very text heavy, but perhaps there was an idea that captive passengers would
be glad of something to read. A 1946 brochure released by the airline in
conjunction with the Irish Tourist Board is a standard of its time: 'Dublin to
the first time visitor, looks semi-American, semi-European. Its broad streets
and its architecture are continental. Its restaurants and lounge-bars follow the
fashion of the great western country (where so many of its exiles stayed).
Most astonished comment of our recent visitors, mostly uniformed, was "can
I have steak?" You can! And lashings of agricultural food.' While this was a
specific promotional ploy, aimed at those British visitors still suffering from
wartime rationing, the idea that Ireland was at once American, and yet
Continental, and underpinned by its rural and historic heritage, would be a
common theme in the years ahead.

One of the first major state initiatives to boost tourism was the An Tóstal
festival that began in 1953. It was inspired by discussions between the government and Pan Am, and would eventually take the form of a series of events
around the country including sporting fixtures, arts festivals and tidy town
competitions. The perception of how Americans saw Ireland was revealed in

> *Every day I take pride in having the opportunity to work for an airline that resonates such a wealth of emotions with Irish people worldwide. The shamrock, a beacon calling you home — such a simple emblem on the tail of our aircraft can evoke nostalgia and patriotism.*
>
> Mark Giles, Ground Operations

early discussions between Pan Am and civil servants in the Department of Industry and Commerce. One of the airline's suggestions was that 'a special national park be created which might be called the Valley of the Fairies or the Home of the Leprechauns ... scarcely an Irish programme on television, radio or in the theatre passes without some allusion to Irish fairies (the wee people), with the result that the leprechaun has been made world famous throughout the generations in song and story'. The national park, it was suggested, would be built next to the terminal at Shannon airport, and that it could be the first thing tourists would see when they arrived in Ireland. The idea was rejected by the government, and An Tóstal was organised as a more honest reflection of 1950s Ireland, rather than the recreation of a stage version of Irishness. For those, including Aer Lingus, involved in selling Ireland, especially in the North American market, they had to create a tourist image that would bring the country to mind, but without resorting to the clichés of paddywhackery. Leprechauns had to be avoided at all cost! An Tóstal was, however, important in getting airlines to think about when people travelled and, once in Shannon, where they went from there. It was evident that passenger numbers were at their lowest between October and May, and that any initiative that would lead to an equalisation of passenger load across the year would be important. Also of concern to the Irish, was that of the annual 160,000 passengers flying into Ireland from the United States in the early 1950s, only 10,000 were staying in the country. While this proved that the Irish positioning of Shannon as the gateway to Europe had been a master-stroke, the benefits in terms of tourism were negligible. As debates raged, in

In the 1950s, Aer Lingus was active in promoting Ireland through leaflets extolling the virtues of the country to its passengers. *Let's Go to Ireland* was produced in the mid-1950s, and included advice on where to visit, details of the places from which Aer Lingus flew and the opinion that, 'you will find a welcome everywhere from a kindly, hospitable people, who have an unfailing sense of humour and a sane hierarchy of values, and who have never outgrown that ancient and delightful human weakness known as passing the time of day' (*courtesy of Tony Murray*).

Above: Aer Lingus has frequently used St Patrick's Day, Ireland's national holiday, as a way of promoting the country and themselves. This included regularly flying stewardesses to the United States, where they would take part in parades, as well as in photo opportunities, and appear on radio and television shows. In 1960, these stewardesses were flown to New York to take part in the parade, and are shown here in a publicity shot sheltering from the spring rain.

Opposite: One of the great annual attractions of the 'Dublin Season' was, and remains, the Horse Show. Held each year in August at the RDS Showgrounds in Dublin, the Horse Show was frequently used in Aer Lingus promotions as a way of attracting the equestrian minded to Ireland.

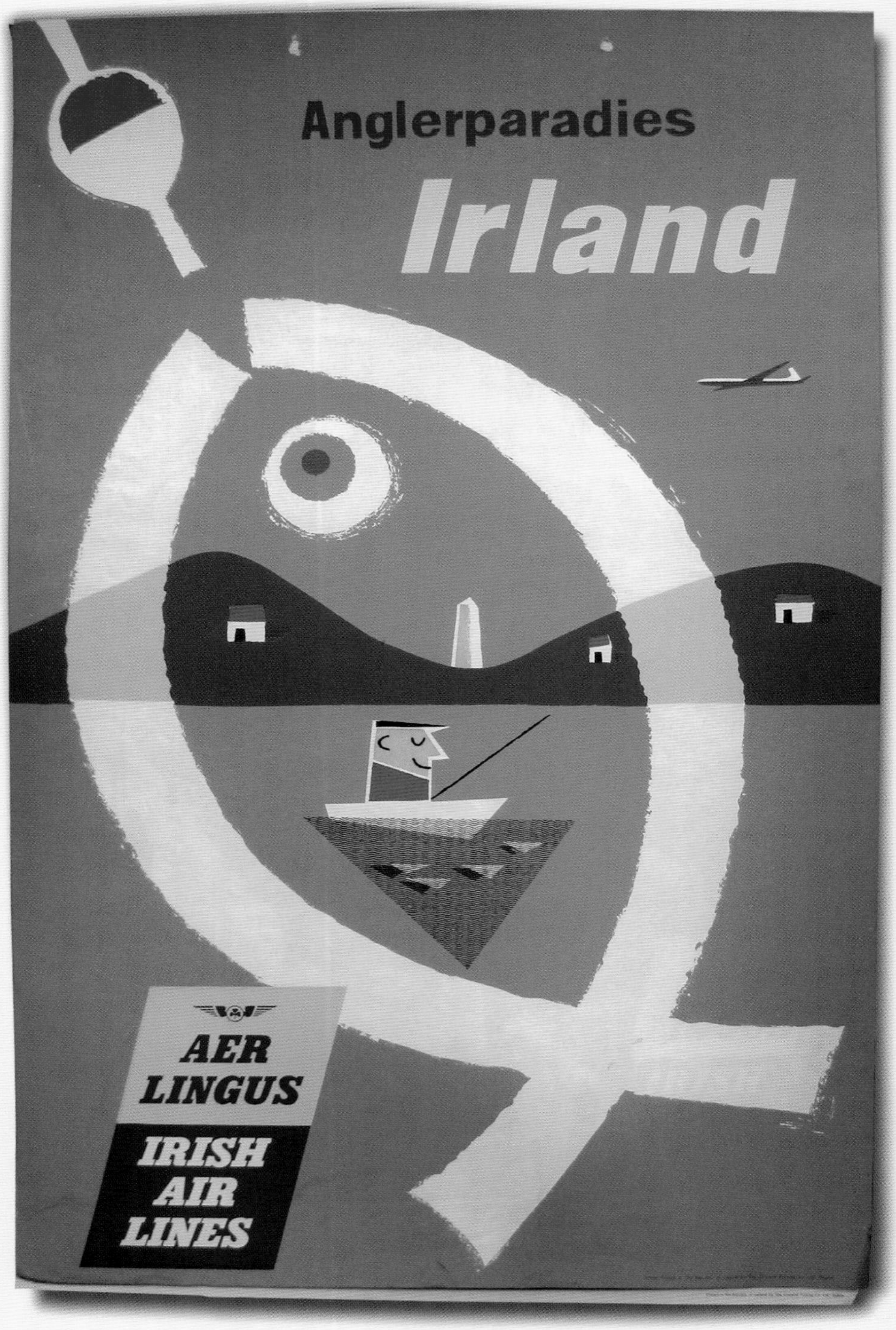
Anglerparadies
Irland
AER
LINGUS
IRISH
AIR
LINES

the 1950s, between the two main Irish political parties as to the desirability of a transatlantic route for Aer Lingus, one thing was clear: if the airline could enter the market as the carrier for traffic into Ireland, and convince passengers to stay in Ireland, they could make a significant impact on tourism numbers.

The Irish Tourist Board, later Bord Fáilte (and now Fáilte Ireland), was originally established in 1924, and primarily concerned with attracting visitors from Britain. In those early years, the dominant image of Ireland, as used in promotional material, was that depicted by Paul Henry. His iconic paintings of mountains, white cottages, turf stacks and the broad skies of Connemara became shorthand visual representations of what Ireland was. It would have been easy for Aer Lingus to stay with such iconic images, but while promoting an Ireland of tradition, the airline was also promoting itself and the inherent modernity of plane travel. As Linda King has shown in her extensive work on Aer Lingus advertising, the decades from the mid-1950s saw the airline develop a strong visual sense of itself and Ireland as a destination. Sun Advertising, who managed the Aer Lingus account from 1951, felt that there was a shortage of talented designers in Ireland. They began recruiting from Holland, in particular individuals who had worked on their KLM account there. Although a formal corporate identity would not emerge at the airline until 1974, the work of Sun Advertising, and their imported designers, would allow Aer Lingus to create a strong brand that sold Ireland overseas. Poster and advertising campaigns shifted from traditional images of rural scenes and embraced concepts from modern art and visual culture to promote a wide range of ideas such as the nation as a place to visit, fishing and other pursuits as something to do, and Aer Lingus itself as a modern, full service airline that

For many anglers around the world, Ireland is a fishing Mecca. Fishing was identified early on by tourist advisors as a key means of attracting tourists to the country. This iconic poster, produced by Sun Advertising, was a modernist take on a traditional pastime, and marked out the airline's advertising campaigns in the 1950s and 1960s as cutting edge.

would get people to their destination quickly and in the utmost comfort. With the shamrock visible on the planes, an ever expanding number of routes and a constantly renewed fleet of modern planes, Aer Lingus was establishing itself through the 1960s as *the* carrier into Ireland.

The decision to heavily market Ireland as a destination, alongside Aer Lingus as a carrier, was a conscious choice made by the airline, and one which dovetailed with government policy towards promoting tourism. In 1963, the General Manager of Aer Lingus, J. F. Dempsey, spoke at a major conference in Dublin where he addressed the issue of how the airline contributed to selling Ireland. He outlined how, in the previous year, Aer Lingus had spent £30,000 of its revenue advertising in Britain, and a further £560,000 in the United States. He argued that other airlines flying into Ireland promoted themselves, rather than the country as a destination (a charge he also levelled at the railway and ferry companies), and that it was only Aer Lingus that had an interest in promoting Ireland. Dempsey argued that Aer Lingus was different, as the money it spent was on 'the encouragement of traffic into Ireland. That is exclusively our theme … Only one airline will ever devote resources to developing Irish tourist traffic and that is Irish International Airways [Aer Lingus].' One fact that Dempsey was keen to highlight was the amount that each tourist spent once in Ireland: £22 for each visitor from Britain, and £45 for each from America. His argument was simple, the more money that the airline spent promoting Ireland, the greater its passenger load and, as a result, an associated increase in tourists who would spend their money in the state.

Publicity for Aer Lingus and Ireland as a destination took a variety of forms.

One of the great attractions of Ireland, for many visitors, is its sporting life. Whether as participants on the golf course and elsewhere, or whether as spectators at race meetings, GAA matches and the like, sport has always encouraged tourists to come. The central place of major horse races in the Irish calendar was a major attraction, particularly to visitors from Britain, and races such as the 1963 Derby were a common feature in airline advertising.

IRISH
SWEEPS
DERBY
1963
Fly
AER LINGUS
IRISH INTERNATIONAL AIRLINES
ESTIMATED VALUE OF RACE £60,000
RUN AT THE CURRAGH JUNE 29TH

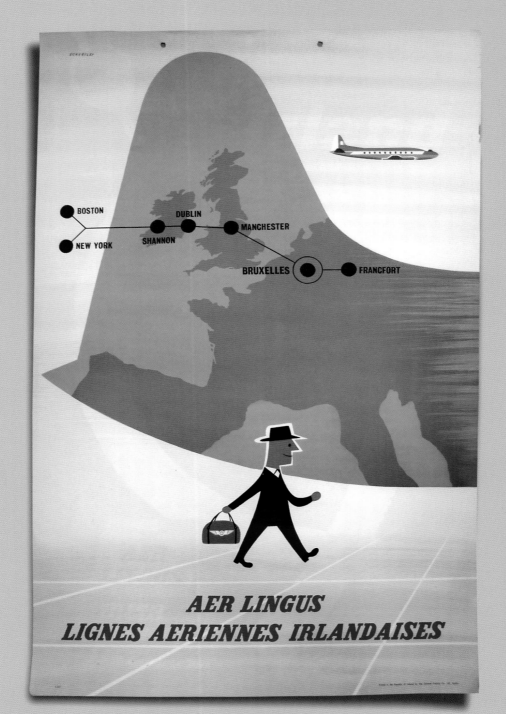

BOSTON

NEW YORK

SHANNON

DUBLIN

MANCHESTER

BRUXELLES

FRANCFORT

**AER LINGUS
LIGNES AERIENNES IRLANDAISES**

The tradition of striking posters that had begun in the 1950s continued until the 1980s when other media, particularly television, took over. The advent of holiday and travel magazines and supplements was a boon to Ireland, and the country was regularly featured as a place to visit for its scenery, people and relaxed way of life. In the United States, the most important such title was *Holiday*, and in its pages Ireland was often lauded. In 1963, there was the first special issue of *Holiday* that concentrated solely on Ireland, and one in which Aer Lingus placed a number of adverts. With the help of Bord Fáilte, Aer Lingus was constantly placing itself in advertising and promotional opportunities as the means of flying to Ireland. Much of this publicity, especially in the United States market, relied on an appeal to traditional views of Ireland, and the desire for emigrants to return home. It was in the emigrant market that Aer Lingus were most active, until the 1990s, in promoting Ireland. The annual Irish festival of St Patrick's Day was a key promotional opportunity, and from 1958, Aer Lingus stewardesses were dispatched to New York and other major cities to take part in the annual parade. In 1959, the airline made a big splash by importing fresh Irish shamrock to New York for distribution. This was not any old shamrock, but that which had been grown on Irish soil, picked the day before and flown to the United States. By taking part so visibly in parades on St Patrick's Day, a pattern that eventually spread across the world, Aer Lingus and its crews planted itself firmly at the heart of the idea of being Irish. Throughout the 1960s and 1970s, flying Aer Lingus staff to St Patrick's Day parades was an aggressive part of the airline's promotional work. As Tom Kennedy, head of press and public relations in North America, recalled: 'Aer Lingus used to bring over for St Patrick's Day about a hundred air and ground hostesses whom we would disperse throughout the United States and

In the late 1950s and early 1960s, Aer Lingus' opening of its transatlantic route, combined with its use of freedom rights in Britain, meant that it connected Europe and the United States through Dublin and Shannon. Such connections, while useful for those who wished to traverse the northern hemisphere, were essential in casting a wide net over potential tourist markets.

Much of the poster art conceived to promote Ireland to foreign tourists was designed in such a way that it could be constantly adapted. Here an advertisement for the German market, promoting the friendly airline, was also used in other languages. While the cartoon bird, sitting on an aircraft wing with its sprig of shamrock were reproduced, the text was translated into various languages for different markets.

In modern tourism marketing language, the cultural or heritage tourist is a key target. People who travel to different cities and countries to consume the arts, festivals and heritage are more likely to be of substance, spend more and stay longer. Before such visitors were identified in such contemporary ways, Aer Lingus was fulsome in its support of artistic events such as the Dublin Theatre Festival.

Canada. No governor of a State, no mayor of a major city, no cardinal, archbishop or bishop with the slightest hint of Irish in his background could escape the green net we threw over the continent. The publicity was literally priceless.'

Linking the North American diaspora with Ireland, via the airline, was part of one of Aer Lingus' most successful advertising campaigns of the 1960s. A map of Ireland was distributed across media outlets in the United States, illustrated with various Irish family names. The strapline on the advert read: 'Will all those listed below please come home for the holidays.' It sparked the imagination, and debate. People from across the United States wrote to the airline demanding to know why their family name had not been included. Eventually, to correct all the omissions, the advert ran into four different printings, but in the process had engaged the diaspora with home, and positioned Aer Lingus as the way to get there.

In 1968, Aer Lingus introduced its in-flight magazine *Cara*. While not unusual in the world of aviation, *Cara* was, until the 2000s, highly focused on selling Ireland above anything else. Nowadays, the magazine reflects the multitude of routes the airline flies to, and features articles on the attractions of cities from Chicago to Barcelona. Prior to this shift there were few articles that dealt with anything apart from the joys of visiting Ireland. Features regularly returned to the delights of Ireland's major cities, the nation's heritage, the different ways of seeing the island (by bike, horse-drawn caravan, on foot or by car), the splendid golf courses and great fishing, and the hidden gems traditionally off the tourist trail such as Leitrim or Roscommon. And it was not simply the editorial content of the magazine. Opening a copy of *Cara* from

While many tourists travel to Ireland with images of the rural, western landscape in their mind, for a great many it is the capital city, Dublin, which brings them here. Aer Lingus has always been a keen advocate of the city and its attractions, and from the earliest days of its advertising campaigns, whether in photograph or as here, in artistic form, Dublin is promoted as a place to visit.

DUBLIN

FLY THERE BY
AER LINGUS
IRISH AIR LINES

cara

The Inflight Magazine of Aer Lingus

Volume 19, No 5.
September/October 1986
Your copy to take away

A town like Athy
Skiing both ways
The greening of Boston
Vanishing Dubliners

AER LINGUS-IRISH

Cara magazine has been a central part of the in-flight experience since its inception. Until the 2000s, the key role of the magazine was to sell the charms of Ireland to the passengers. Leading journalists, writers, photographers and artists were commissioned for the magazine and often they chose to highlight, as here with Athy, places from off the usual tourist trail.

the 1980s, for example, there are large colour adverts for the Switzers department stores ('one of Ireland's great attractions'), Field's Jewellers ('bring home only the best'), House of Ireland ('home to the treasures of Ireland'), Kilkenny Stores ('Castles, Clothes, Crafts and Coffee'), Avoca ('the beginning of an Irish legend'), Jury's hotels ('traditional hospitality'), Clery's ('a legend in shopping') and the Industrial Development Authority ('we're the young Europeans'). The magazine, which has been read by millions as they sat on board, promotes Ireland and all it has to offer as a tourist destination, as well as a place for investors. For those arriving in Ireland it gives them pointers for what they might do, for those leaving, it tells them what they have missed, and perhaps encourages them to return.

Alongside the on-board selling of Ireland through the pages of *Cara*, the traditions of Irish hospitality embodied by the cabin crew and the Irishness of what was served and sold on board, Aer Lingus was also active, particularly from the 1980s, in television advertising. While many of its North American advertisements sold Ireland as a place to visit, there was also a strong strand of selling Ireland as home. This was most famously evident in the 1980s series of commercials titled 'You're home'. This has been a key device in all Aer Lingus' selling of the nation. Ireland may be the physical home that you are aiming for, but once on board your Aer Lingus flight, whether from New York, London or Rome, the skill of the airline was to make you feel that you were already at home. The planes functioned as a little bit of Ireland in the sky.

In the 1990s, the tourist market for Ireland shifted away from its traditional dependence on the North American market due to the aftershocks in the travel industry of the Gulf War, and began turning its attention more fully to the British and European markets. The airline worked closely with Fáilte Ireland to capture the new generation of city break travellers, and they were successful in marketing Dublin as a trendy place to spend a weekend. Major sporting events such as the Ryder Cup, in 2006, and the success of Irish provincial rugby teams and the national soccer team, were also important for selling Ireland overseas, and Aer Lingus advertising has constantly stressed the pleasures of the country as a sporting site.

In 2009, the income generated from tourism in Ireland was valued at €3

Aer Lingus ☘

cara

MARCH/APRIL 1998   VOLUME 31   NO. 2

JOHN HINDE
Postcards from
the Edge

BOSTON
Revolutionary City

PENSIONS
Leaping into
Retirement

YOUR COMPLIMENTARY COPY

Left: The success of *Cara* and its reach, in terms of readership, has made it a successful part of Aer Lingus' marketing strategy. It has always remained at the cutting edge of magazine design, and visually reflects the styles of high-end publishing. In the 1990s, while Ireland and its imagery was still foregrounded – including this red-haired woman in the West from 1998 – it was also turning its attention to those other cities to which the airline flew.

Above: In the 1990s, the number of flights and routes flown by Aer Lingus increased dramatically. The *Bringing Ireland to the World* campaign of 1995 was a way of selling Ireland and the connections between the country and beyond.

billion. Of the millions of passengers Aer Lingus flew on its various routes that year, a large percentage were heading to Ireland for their holidays, whether a two-week jaunt through the west of Ireland or forty-eight hours of fun in Dublin. Aer Lingus has always functioned, because of its readily recognisable brand as the Irish airline, as a flag carrier for Ireland as a destination. As Tom Kennedy stated in 1986, after three decades of promoting Aer Lingus and Ireland in North America, 'one of the things I always felt about working for Aer Lingus was that all the time you were being a patriot'. Selling the airline and selling Ireland were, and remain, indivisible.

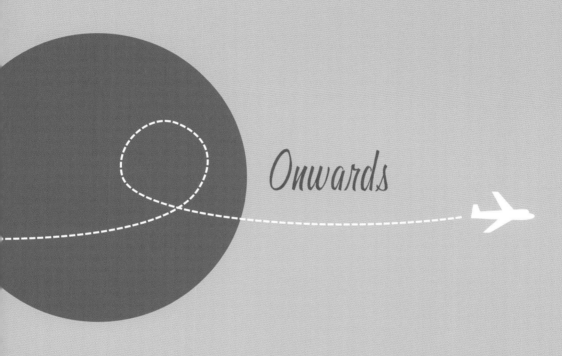

Onwards

The airline industry will continue to change and develop in the coming decades. There will be new challenges for Aer Lingus, but after seventy-five years it looks back on a fascinating history. It started life as the flag carrier of a small, newly independent nation, and only flew as far as the country next door. It has grown its routes, business and passenger numbers, so that it now works as the only airline that can connect Ireland with the world through its network and partnerships with other airlines. For the millions of people who have flown Aer Lingus over the decades, there will be a million different memories. Whether flying for business or pleasure, emigrating or returning, Aer Lingus has been instrumental in moving people through the skies. Older travellers will remember smaller planes, with a more intimate service. Others might recall the size and scale of the jumbo jets that used to traverse the Atlantic. An exclusive group will recall the comfort and opulence of first class travel. As our concept of what flying entails has changed, so our expectations of airlines have transformed. Today Aer Lingus works as a full service carrier across the Atlantic and as a competitive economy carrier on its short haul routes. For the passenger today, our need is to get efficiently, and cheaply, from A to B. We expect good service and comfort, but perhaps no longer require the pampering and personalised service of early travellers. However, where Aer Lingus differs from many of its competitors in a highly competitive aviation industry is that it is perceived as having a clear identity: it is the Irish airline. This is not simply a product of green uniforms and shamrock logos, but a product of Aer Lingus' history.

The airline was developed and has been supported by the state, as a sign

Courtesy of Piotr Wargacki

Aer Lingus means Ireland. Whenever I step aboard, I already feel like I've arrived on the Emerald Isle.

Mary Langon, Reservations, New York

of Ireland's modernity and nationhood. It has represented Ireland in the skies, on the streets of St Patrick's Day parades, on television and across the globe in its training and management of other airlines. Aer Lingus has flown the Irish people, its diapsora and others to a multitude of destinations. It has carried sports teams, pop stars, beauty queens, presidents, pandas and a Pope, and all of them have understood that they were on board an Irish airline. A key strength of the airline is its staff. While industrial relations are always complex, and there have been periods when those who work for the airline have expressed their discontent, it is obvious, when reading the back issues of *Aer Scéala* or talking to staff, past and present, that there is a great deal of pride connected with working for Aer Lingus. That pride translates itself to the job that people do across the airline, and in the service that they provide. Whatever the future may hold, and no matter the challenges that lie ahead, the history of Aer Lingus is an important part of the story of the nation. While we, as passengers, may rush through the airport to take our seats on board, perhaps we should take a moment to reflect on the past. Our modern aircraft is a product of constant updating, purchasing and technological innovation. The personnel who book seats, move bags, service planes, ensure their timely departure, pilot them and serve us are the result of decades of training and innovation. And most of all, the green-liveried, shamrock tailfinned plane is a testament to the visionaries of 1936 and a symbol of Aer Lingus and Ireland.

Index

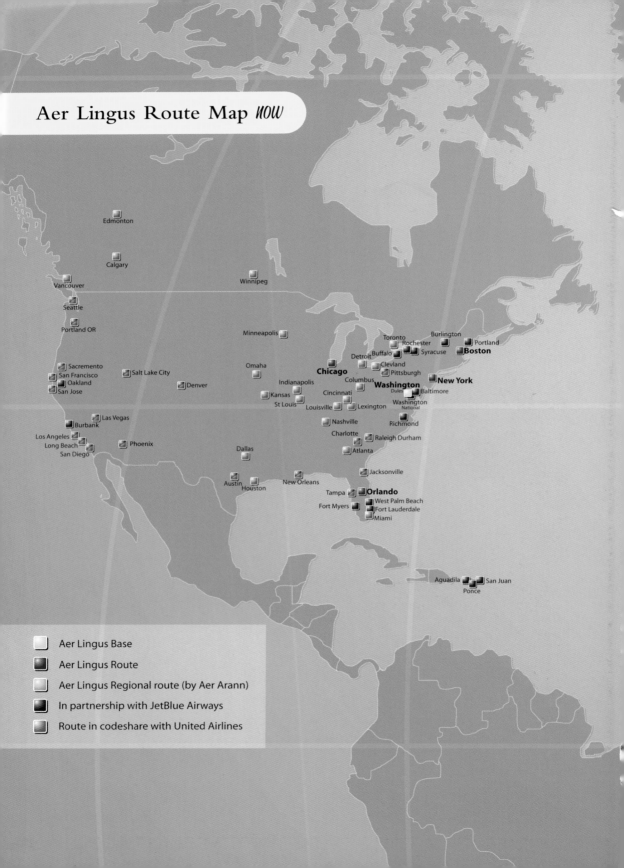

Aer Lingus Route Map *NOW*

Edmonton

Calgary

Vancouver

Seattle

Portland OR

Winnipeg

Minneapolis

Sacramento
San Francisco
Oakland
San Jose

Salt Lake City

Omaha

Denver

Las Vegas

Burbank

Los Angeles
Long Beach
San Diego

Phoenix

Indianapolis

Kansas

St Louis

Chicago

Columbus

Cincinnati

Louisville

Lexington

Detroit

Cleveland

Pittsburgh

Toronto
Buffalo

Rochester

Syracuse

Burlington

Portland

Boston

New York

Washington

Dulles

Baltimore

Washington
National

Nashville

Charlotte

Raleigh Durham

Richmond

Dallas

Austin
Houston

New Orleans

Tampa

Fort Myers

Orlando

West Palm Beach

Fort Lauderdale

Miami

Atlanta

Jacksonville

Aguadila

Ponce

San Juan

	Aer Lingus Base
	Aer Lingus Route
	Aer Lingus Regional route (by Aer Arann)
	In partnership with JetBlue Airways
	Route in codeshare with United Airlines